TWO EQUALS ONE

STEVE COPPARD

Copyright © 2024 by Steve Coppard

All rights reserved.

No part of this book may be reproduced in any form or by any electronic or mechanical means, including information storage and retrieval systems, without written permission from the author, except for the use of brief quotations in a book review.

1
THE END, POSSIBLY

Linda, my best friend and dearest wife of thirty one years, I have decided to take up writing as a kind of therapy to cope with losing you. Two strong reasons drive this. Firstly, we had so many wonderful adventures in beautiful places with cock-ups galore, that need to be preserved. Secondly, grief is such a taboo subject and most people are totally unprepared to face it. I hope that by telling our tale it may help others in some way.

Style... Well, we both know I don't have any! But I know we loved our endless hours in the summerhouse, surrounded by our myriad of holiday souvenirs, chatting about adventures we've had and planning the next one. So I am writing this as though we are in our wicker chairs, a bottle of white wine on the table between us, just chatting away. I hope it works.

So here goes.

If you are really fortunate in life, you will meet that one person whose thoughts and ways comfortably entwine with yours so perfectly that they become as much a part of you as your own body and soul.

Who would think of a divorce party as an occasion that would transform two lives? Some would say our meeting was a typical start to what many would think of as our unconventional life together. Linda and Steve, oh the adventures we had! The (mainly) highs and thankfully few lows we encountered, as we came to realise we were made for each other. If only we had been allowed a few more years, my darling.

As the only two partygoers who smoked, you and I spent the evening outside the kitchen door, with the dustbin for company. We talked, smoked and drank copious amounts of rough Bulgarian Bulls Blood red wine.

Somehow, we bonded. There might have been a touch of desperation in the situation as well; we were both in our early thirties, I was certainly lonely, and you too I think, Lin. Although you had many friends, you were also seeking a soul-mate.

Steve and Linda were now a couple.

In later years, you would refer to us as 'Two old socks' – one no good without the other. How right you were, even though I did need a little darning in the beginning!

We were an unlikely pairing, but surprisingly we had lived our early lives barely half a mile apart, in the suburb of Hangleton in the northern area of Hove near Brighton. Me in the council estate and you in your family's house near the shops. We even frequented many of the same haunts, but not being in the same schools we had a different set of friends. I think we confounded a few people, not least our parents, by making it work, and didn't we just, my darling.

The adventures and travels we enjoyed over 31 years of marriage is too good a tale not to put into writing. As in life, there is sadness too, but overwhelmingly the memories are of good times and a togetherness that I will certainly never find again.

The 28th October 2021 was the day two old socks became one, and you were right Lin – one is no good without the other.

That damn cancer finally got you, too late in diagnosis in this Covid-riddled decade. Your beloved sister Sara held one hand and I the other as you slipped away peacefully.

We knew it would happen, but a couple more years together would have been a time we could have cherished. At least it did allow us to plan things together, the will, the service, your guests, even your music.

It could not have gone better. The sun shone, your wonderful lifelong friends, and more were there, around seventy in all. Having friends Andy (Andrea) and Adrian hosting the service worked beautifully. Your nephew, Tom, read a poem. Then all back to the Windmill, our local, where they did us proud.

2

CORFU: HOW IT ALL BEGAN

The TV program, 'A Place in the Sun', was just on. Yes dear, I still watch that damn program every day! Even the repeats, which shows how dire the TV is. Johny Irwin, our favourite presenter, died last week. Bloody cancer got him, of course. He was so young, and a family man too... Tragic. Anyhow, Corfu was the destination, and it made me stop and think how much we owed that wonderful island in the sun. Without it we would never have met. I'd been on a week's holiday to Arillas, with my cousin Howard for company. We spent most of our time in The Flamingo; a bar/restaurant that had a pool overlooking the beach. It was a new establishment and the owners, Sophocles and Aleko, didn't really have any idea how to market the place to British tourists. They didn't even know what to put on the menu. I helped draw up some signs and gave them a few ideas for food options. Sophocles and I got on really well. When my week was up, they said if I wanted to stay and help them for their first season, I could have a job! Hmm... tempting.

Back home, I started to wonder if I should have stayed out in Corfu. Arillas was such a lovely, unspoilt place; I had grand ideas about launching the resort as a relaxing place to de-stress for executives. Of course, I had no funds, so it was a pipe dream. I was a just a jobbing mechanic, working wherever I could. The more I thought about The Flamingo Bar, the more it pulled me in. When I phoned Sophocles and said I was thinking of taking up his offer, he was overjoyed; apparently Aleko and his wife Harrula were a formidable duo, and tried to dismiss any of his ideas for making the place more welcoming. At this point, alarm bells should have rung... I asked if I could bring anything over for them, as many Western products were very expensive in Greece, back in 1998. Soph asked for music CDs, while Aleko wanted a socket set, spark plugs and filters for his aging Alfa Romeo. So off I set – Lord knows what the Customs Officers thought of my suitcase! It was mid June and I had a return flight booked for two weeks later, in case I'd made a mistake.

Arriving at the Flamingo, the welcome I got from Soph and the barman Janni allayed my fears. Aleko was aloof, as always. Sophocles had a rented two bedroom villa ten minutes' walk away on the road out of town, so I could bunk down there. Aleko and Harrula lived in a small caravan on site; boy, that must have got hot! I loved that place. My first job every day was to sluice down the paving around the pool, and wipe clean the edges above the waterline. Being ever inventive, I quickly found that the best way to do this was astride a Lilo in the pool! I would slop buckets of water up over the side to de-dust the paving, wiping the edges as I went. Hardly work, and it served as my daily wash! The sea water pool was fed from a pipe that ran under the road and fifty metres out into the sea. For my three months there I had a permanent 'salt crust' but I don't think I was stinky... No-one ever said, anyway! My wages were always a bit vague. I got some cash each week, mainly for cigarettes and booze, and was told that Aleko was saving the rest for my end-of-season payoff. Idiot! I also did bar work and helped with the catering. Originally, they were trying to do a labour-intensive Taverna-type menu, without much success. I suggested a self-service buffet at lunchtimes, under the awning overlooking the pool. With two plate sizes, and two prices, it took off and was so much easier to manage. It was my job to run it, and explain the set up to tourists. I'd found that in the village, tasty corn cobs were being sold as chicken feed. It took some persuading to get Aleko to add them to the buffet, but people loved them! And Aleko loved the price. Most guests enjoyed the buffet, being able to choose and help themselves – all except the Italians, who stubbornly refused to adopt self-service, and sat by the pool until they either relented, or left. They were often very rude.

For my food, I usually cooked myself a frozen Moussaka with some baked beans. I pretty much lived on one of those a day, so I soon slimmed down, and with a deep tan I felt better than I had done in years. I was quite enjoying myself – except when Soph's wife and daughter came to visit, because I was relegated to sleeping in the beer cellar! I piled towels on a sunbed, lit two anti-mosquito coils and tried to ignore my thousand winged bedfellows. Surprisingly, my salt crust seemed to deter the mozzies, but I couldn't wait to return to the villa. One morning, I emerged from the cellar to the sound of splashing and laughter; three young guys were fooling around in the pool. I walked over to tell them that we weren't open yet, and the tall one said, "What's up, Youth?" The Hod Wads had landed. The tall one, Dave, was a submariner in the Navy. His mate Mark worked in a car factory in Coventry, and Dave's younger brother was working on a building site. I can't recall his name, as they only ever called him 'Youth'. In normal circumstances, this trio would have horrified me, but they were really friendly and I warmed to them. I told them to sit quietly on the top terrace while I made them a mug of tea, as Aleko was still asleep. They were here for a week, but to save their cash for drinking, they'd brought a tent and pitched it in the dunes next to the Flamingo. I knew Sophocles would like the guys, but I did think that Aleko would ban them. But they bought breakfast every day, and a meal, and drank like fish. Money being Alekos religion, he overlooked their exuberance. I befriended them and showed them the local sites on my couple of hours off each day. There was a traditional old Taverna up the high street, not at all touristy, so of course we loved it. Now, the proprietor was a lovely old boy who used to brew his own wine. He called it 'Grassi' – that might just be a slang word, but he used to let us buy a gallon of it at a time, on condition that I didn't sell it at the Flamingo. It was a little cloudy, slightly fizzy and bloody lovely. We would sit on the beach, swigging out of the flagon, after which we would return to the Flamingo to perfect our synchronised swimming routine! No, don't ask...

Perhaps I should explain why the boys were called 'The Hod Wads'. It was a phrase they used to say many times a day, which seemed to refer to the building trade. 'Hod, Wad, Spod, Shovel, Dumper Truck, Youth!' I think it was about the extraordinary sums of money that Dave's brother picked up as a hod carrier, and that he could have been worse off digging (Spod = Spade, or Shovel), but life would have been easier as a dumper truck driver... Well, that's my interpretation! Each morning, the guys walked up the high street to the shop to get their cigarettes. They told me that a small boy always greeted them with a Greek phrase, and they often gave him some coins. I translated; 'Good morning…' and then his name for them. Let's just say, it rhymes with bankers! I was very sad to see the boys depart, but I had their phone numbers and vowed to keep in touch. And we did!

One night, in a violent storm, a sailing boat broke loose from its moorings and was being driven towards the rocky beach west of the Flamingo. The German holiday rep who owned it begged us all to help him get on board, so he could start the motor and get it back to the pier. A group of us got in the water to keep it off the rocks; he saved his boat, and we were all glad to have helped. Rescuing that boat would pay dividends at the end of the season, as the rep gave me a lift to stay with friends in Bavaria, on my convoluted route home. There were always new regulars pitching up at the Flamingo. One couple, Moira and Jim, were to be the catalyst for our first meeting, my dearest Linda. Moira and Jim lived in Brighton, only a few miles from my family home. Knowing that my mother was quite anxious about how I was doing, I asked if they might call on her to set her mind at rest. On their return they kindly did that for me, and it was the start of a good friendship. It was Moira and Jim that invited me to the fateful divorce party of their friend Anne. That, my dear, is of course where we met. We felt an instant mutual attraction; it truly was our destiny to be together.

By the end of July, Aleko was starting to wonder if I was earning my keep. I suspect it might have been because I'd started hiding my cigarettes, so he couldn't steal them. Sophocles suggested I try and come up with an idea to boost the catering profits, so the Corfu Sunday roast was born. Surprisingly good beef joints could be had in Corfu town, and I phoned my mother for advice on how to replicate her fantastic high-rise Yorkshire puddings. That, and how to make crispy roast potatoes! I demonstrated the technique to a very dubious Aleko and Harrula. I did wonder if olive oil would work for the potatoes, but Aleko expertly mixed the oil with a little water and to my amazement it worked fine. Desert would be apple pie and ice cream. Proper gravy proved to be a real issue, until I found a catering tin of Bisto in a cash and carry in the capital. The meal was an instant success. We were serving around twenty people every Sunday evening, much to the owners' shock! Back home in the winter, Birdseye ran a TV advert for braised beef as part of a roast dinner, for two tanned tourists back from holiday. The tag line was ' You can't get that in Corfu!' Boy, did I shout at the TV.

Towards the middle of September, things started quieting down. There were a few rainy days and we prepared to close the place up for the winter. This did mean that Soph and I got a bit of free time to explore, so he took me to some wonderful village tavernas and ordered delicious food that I would not normally try. One Saturday afternoon we went to some kind of festival. It was lively chaos, with traditional music and dancing – for all I know, we might have gate crashed a wedding. My overriding memory is of a whole spit of roast lamb, served in a pitta bread – delicious! Sophocles also took me to a beach bar on the east coast, owned by a friend of his from Thessaloniki on the mainland. There was a downstairs bar and terrace and a snack bar on the first floor with a frontage open to sea views. A small bedsit was behind the upstairs serving counter. Soph sang my praises and his friend asked me if I wanted to run it for him next season! Wow. Darling, that would be my choice the following spring – Corfu or you, my dear! Thank goodness you won.

By October, I was ready to leave. I gave my German friend a share of the ferry fare to Ancona in Italy and looked forward to the journey through the mountains, to visit my friends in

Rosenheim. Aleko paid me the remainder of my wages; not quite what I was expecting, but they do say 'Never trust a Greek'. After an emotional farewell with Sophocles, I was off.

I couldn't believe how wonderfully beautiful and majestic the Alps were. I instantly fell for the place. My friends, Michael and Sabine, were excellent hosts to this bedraggled, scruffy, ill-equipped traveller. We'd met on a holiday to Rhodes and been penfriends ever since, exchanging annual Christmas parcels of our respective countries' seasonal treats.

Michael gave me a green coat, which I loved, as I was not really dressed for the alpine Autumn. They introduced me to their friends and showed me the sights; Gros Glockner, the magnificent high alpine road, Salzburg, Munich, and many magical mountain lakes and towns. One of their friends, Elizabeth, took me on a trek to an Alm, the wonderful rest stops for hikers. Amidst green pastures and clanging cow bells, we ate a hearty soup with chunks of warm fresh bread. She was a volunteer with the mountain rescue service, and managed to arrange a flight in their search and rescue plane. Called The Optica, it could fly at low speeds like a helicopter, and its cockpit was a bulbous Perspex bubble for all-round vision. It was an absolutely fantastic experience, weaving in and out of the snowy peaks. The Bavarian hospitality was boundless. I was so grateful, especially as by then I must have looked like a tramp, with my clothes literally falling apart. It was time to head home. I was just about broke; I'd hoped to find work on a big American airbase in the area, but I couldn't even get in the gate. Hod Wad Mark came to my rescue; he posted me £100 to help me get home.

A lot of trucks came on the Autobahn through the nearby pass from Italy, stopping at the big motorway service centre en-route. I decided that's where I would try to hitch a lift north, as I'd heard that drivers' mates get free ferry passage. Sabine dropped me off there on her way to work. After an hour with barely a truck passing, I went in for a coffee. A kindly waitress practiced her English on me, and informed me it was a national holiday in Italy. Trucks might be scarce, but she was just finishing her shift and she offered to give me a lift to Sabine's office. I think Sabine's face dropped when I walked in. I explained the situation, and her solicitor boss said, "Take him to Munich Station and buy him a ticket north!" I felt terrible, but I really was in a tricky situation. Sabine put me on a train to Hamburg, saying there was a ferry there. I'd sort of been heading for Calais, or better still Dieppe, but I was grateful just the same. It was about 500 miles; a long way to go with no spare cash. I didn't know how much the ferry would be, so I didn't dare buy anything in case I blew it. But at least I was warm, comfortable and heading north. An elegant lady sitting opposite me started chatting. She was a doctor on her way home to Hannover. I relayed my sorry tale, and when the catering trolley came round she bought me a sandwich and a coffee! The generosity of strangers was quite astounding. Now, darling, thanks to you, money is not an issue, so I too try to be generous when I see an opportunity. Arriving in Hamburg, it was chilly and a shock to the system. The station had a city map, so I worked out a walk to the ferry port. It wasn't too far, and went via the famous (or infamous) Reeperbahn red light district. A notice board told me all I needed to know; the next ferry departed in 36 hours, and a foot passenger fare for the 24-hour crossing was just about in my budget, leaving me £3. Luckily, I'd bought a couple of packets of biscuits before leaving Bavaria, so they would have to do. I went back to the station, hoping for at least a warm bench for the night, but the police were turfing all of us 'vagrants' out. I spent the night on a chilly Park bench, overlooking the ferry port. I was so pleased to get on board, and find out that my fare included a free bunk. I had enough cash for two coffees, so I had to space them out. That was a long voyage! I got talking to another Brit, and blagged a ride south from Harwich. He dropped me off south of London, on the A23. When I put my thumb out in hope, an empty coach stopped. And blow me down, he was passing within half a mile of home! I'd set off in June to make my fortune, so the look on my mother's face when she opened the door to this tramp, said it all. But, Linda, without that roller coaster of a summer, we never would have met. And that would have been tragic. I miss you, darling.

3
COPING?

Now, six weeks after we laid you to rest, I am on a cruise ship – P&O's Ventura, our home for so many adventures. I am hoping it might help to get my head straight after the wonderful service and the endless paperwork that is required when a loved one dies. That's a horrible word, so final, but of course you are in my thoughts and mind every waking minute. We've had so many good times together that I must now use these great memories to wash over more recent images.

It's been a bumpy ride so far. A storm is following us down through the Bay of Biscay, bad enough to cancel our stop in Vigo. We're sheltering for two days in Lisbon, a city we loved; the boat trip and coach tour, wandering the squares... You tripping over and having to wear a moon boot for a month! It could only happen to you my darling, but you did enjoy the two hunky crewmen helping you get up!

I think this trip is doing me good, giving me time to try and get my head straight. I am only eating in the buffet, I cannot bring myself to sit at a big table and be sociable. I spend a lot of time in the panoramic bar, Metropolis, that sits across the stern with great views. Sometimes the memories overwhelm me and I sit sobbing to myself. Human nature being what it is, most people avoid me like the plague, but if they have endured a tragedy in their lives, they recognise it in me and stop to ask if they can help. Some people are lovely.

I have been catching quite a few of the shows, the early ones anyway. At least there is a lot going on. Of course, I have been drinking way too much – and gambling, you know how I like the roulette.

I played bingo on the first two sea days, and for the first time I won a line prize on both days! Amazing.

As for the casino... Well, as expected, I lost in the first half of the cruise, very nearly using up all the cash I had allowed for gambling, I won't say how much darling, I don't want you turning over!

But the second half of the trip I could do no wrong, winning every day, to the extent that I paid off most of my cruise account and came off the ship with the same amount of cash I got on with. I think you may have been guiding the roulette ball when you saw how much I was losing at first!

I only went ashore in places we had not visited together, to avoid (though that sounds horrible), the memories. But I needed some time to chill. I had short wanders in Cartagena and Malaga, two beers on the front in the first and some trinket shopping and a beer in Malaga. In Gibraltar, I just went down the gangplank to the duty-free shop and got a litre of gin and Spanish brandy. Cleverly, the brandy was in a luggage-friendly oblong plastic bottle.

Ventura was only running at around forty percent occupancy, which was actually very pleasant, but the Covid hoops you had to go through to get on board and return home again were very wearing.

I disembarked with a folder of certificates and documents, down the gangplank, luggage in hand (getting too old for this!), through the customs hall and straight to the car park. Not an official in sight, even for the passport! Unbelievable.

As for Christmas and New Year, the least said the better.

Last year, 2021, was the year from hell. You spent most of December 2020 in Hospital, and during Christmas week you were up in Stanmore having your hip rebuilt. No visitors allowed, it was a nightmare! But they did stop the agony you had endured for months, my brave girl. The day I picked you up from there and bought you home was one of the happiest days I have known, just to have you back was wonderful.

Your new £5.5k stair lift was ready and waiting, but at least you could be in your beloved home. The journey through cancer was just beginning.

4

MEMORIES

Hey, remember our first ever trip together, to Normandy in that battered and highly illegal Ford Capri of mine?

The summer before we met, I had worked in Corfu, and had been offered another job supposedly running a beach bar in a different resort (although I suspect I would have ended up as the 'dogsbody' again).

I worked at Unigate Dairies back then, as a mechanic, and had this old Capri that I was doing up to drive back to Greece in the summer. Hand-painted black it was, mechanically sound, but a heap none the less. You had a perfectly nice Renault 5, but we took my old wreck over to Dieppe via Newhaven for a few days while I decided whether or not to go to Greece. Such was the affect you were having on me!

We had a great time, surprisingly, as we were so naïve it was untrue. We got off the ferry at around 7am, having tried to sleep in the awful reclining chairs. We were poor then, no cabin for us! I drove us to Reims, where we intended to spend a couple of days exploring the ancient city – a supposed 90 minute drive that somehow took me 3 hours.

We found a small hotel and rang the bell, and were a bit taken aback when the owner said, "No, you can't have a room at 10 am!"

I can remember to this day the little café we found around the corner, where we savoured coffee, croissants and fresh gorgeous baguettes for the first time.

We decided to head for the coast, where we had a glorious few days filled with long walks, lovely lunches, and discovering Moules et Frites overlooking the sea.

The thing we both recalled most though was waiting for the ferry home. Sitting in the car on the cliff top above the ferry terminal, drinking orange juice from those little cardboard cartons with a straw in, while being able to get a British radio station. Then you started sucking on the empty carton, making a really annoying noise. I said "stop," but of course you carried on, as you would, so I grabbed it and tossed it out the window! You told me off, and to this day I regret littering those cliff tops.

On returning home, our time together convinced me that you were the one. Corfu was no longer in my future – just you, my wonderful Linda Jayne.

Now, rolling forward, believe it or not I am in a Warner's resort, Lakeside on Hayling Island, trying out a four-night, midweek break. I know we went to one on the Isle of Wight back in 2015, and declared it nice, but ten years too early. But my situation is different now, lonely nights watching crap on the telly and being in bed at nine are becoming tedious, so I thought it would be worth a try. It really is friendly here! I managed to get two good-fitting shirts in the foyer this morning. When I came back after Archery (don't ask! I'm not a natural!), the stall had gone, so I could not get any more. But the resort manager got them to check in the stock room for any more in my huge size. None left, sadly, but talk about going the extra mile. It is actually very nice here, I can see why your dear mum loved it.

There have been a few teary moments the last couple of weeks; the three-month anniversary of your passing, and the day before, when Sandra downstairs gave me a leaflet for your beloved Women's Institute.

On the back was a notice for the Linda Coppard annual trophy, to be awarded to the lady who has achieved the most in the year. Darling, you would be so proud!

It is lovely to know they think so highly of you.

I must say, I am very impressed with Warner's, the Woodland Lodge I am in is very comfortable. There's a huge bed with a nice flat screen television on the wall at the foot of it, a super walk-in shower, and a nice selection of drinks and snacks in the room. Even a fridge containing a pint of fresh milk.

There are plenty of activities throughout the day and shows every night. Even the food is very good, and the lovely staff are the crowning glory.

As the show stage is in the dining room, you are allocated a table in the restaurant/theatre and that table is yours for the duration. There is a nice lady, Marion, on the table next to me, and we've been on a couple of guided walks and had a coffee. But you know me, never a very social soul, I haven't been to any of the shows. It's a Queen tribute act tonight though, so I might make an exception.

You, my dear would have absolutely loved it here. I can see why your mum and dad came here so often, they would have been in their element being such socialites! I wish we'd thought of it for your last summer.

Home tomorrow, I must get stuck in to getting your beloved garden into shape. I have told the family that I hope to plant your special rose, Simply the Best, a dusky orange variety along with your ashes on Easter Saturday.

It was so nice of Andrea to send it down from Scotland especially for this purpose. You have some wonderful friends.

Gail, next door, has found out that cremation ashes are not good for the garden in the growing season. So, my darling, you will be in the summerhouse a while longer, but it was your favourite place.

I have two more trips booked so far, a cottage in Cornwall, near Padstow, in March and a place in Cardigan Bay in April. Both locations were on our wish list for our retirement. I hope I can enjoy the beautiful places on my own, and it does not send me running home in tears like I did in Teignmouth in November 2021. I think that was way too soon for me, a desperate escape that did not work.

5
BENA VISTA

Right, happy thoughts now! I recall how we got into 'Timeshares' back in their heyday in the 1990s. That was down to your wonderful father, Fred. He bought your mother a week or two in Benalmádena on the Costa del Sol, and we were always hearing of their adventures with their old friends, Jill and Pete.

When they said they would use an exchange for a resort near Estepona, and asked if we wanted to come, we were very excited.

Club Bena Vista, on the main coast road between Marbella and Estepona, in 1995 I think it was. They booked a one bedroom unit and we were to share the sofa bed in the lounge. We were young and slim then, so no problem.

We flew out to Malaga, Fred had arranged a hire car and off we went. The coast road wound up the mountainside towards Mijas, when Fred declared, "I need a drink and a pee!" There was an off-ramp with a fuel station and a cafeteria coming up, so I pulled off the motorway. We found a terrace with far reaching views over the coast, and your dad ordered beers and Spanish omelette for all of us. It was a lovely start to our holiday.

Driving into the resort, we were pleased to see it was the traditional white Andalusian village style, with villas off to the west and reception sitting on the first floor above a row of restaurants and small shops. By strange coincidence, the year before on our campervan tour of Iberia we'd stopped at a bar on the opposite side of the road and admired this place.

There was a clubhouse with a pool, two other pools, tennis courts, access to a gym... it looked idyllic. Fred and I went to reception and my eyes widened.

"Dave?" I exclaimed.

"Hi Steve," he replied.

I was amazed. The last time I saw Dave he was managing the Dragons Health Club at the bottom of our road in Hove. He said he saw the resort manager's job advertised and just went for it.

The happy result of his new position was that he gave us adjoining apartments – no sharing, phew!

When we walked in, we fell in love with the place. Cool marble floors, the table laid for dinner, even a bottle of local wine in a wicker basket. The balcony had a charcoal BBQ and Bougainvillea climbed the walls.

By the end of our stay we'd bought a week in March for ourselves, and a couple of years later, a second week in August. We had so many wonderful times there, exploring the Costa del Sol.

6

TRYING TO COPE

Now it's mid-May, a few weeks on. I've found it hard to get my writing head on, I set up the laptop in your beloved summer house but I just could not get it together. Now here I am, back at Warner's on Hayling Island. Now that it's warmer the guests are generally a lot older, and if ever the 'God's waiting room' comment was warranted it is here. A scary glimpse of my fate, perhaps.

I went to Cornwall in March, stayed in a lovely cottage with a log burner, the pub just yards away. The weather was atrocious, rain and gales… When I stopped to take a photo in Boscastle, my lovely suede gloves blew off a bridge over the river and played Pooh Sticks down to the sea! You would have laughed fit to burst! How I wish you could have been here.

I stayed in Warner's Cricket St Thomas for two nights on the way, beautiful house and grounds, but I didn't find it as welcoming as Lakeside. It was huge and sprawling, with long walks from the walled garden rooms to function rooms.

The cottage was lovely, a log burner and a local pub at the end of the terrace, but as always, there were negatives. But then, there always is with me, as you well know, Bongle. The water pressure was dire, the shower a trickle, the tank not big enough for more than two inches of water in the bottom of the bath. The owners advice: 'don't run any water, or flush the loo, to allow the pressure to build up!' The pub shut on Monday and didn't reopen until Friday. I tried three times to park in Padstow – no chance, even in March – and to top it off, it poured down nearly all the time.

But I did enjoy the drives.

All in all, not a great trip.

And then came Wales.

Whatever made me think I needed peace and tranquillity? The lodge was beautiful, high-spec and modern, set in a small farm that provided stables. The sky television box kept crashing and it was 10.4 miles to the only pub that survived lockdown!

The scenery was stunning, but the only people I spoke to were dog walkers, nodding a 'good morning,' and the charming hosts. The drives out were very scenic and the coastal villages charming, but even in this early season it is obvious they cannot cope with the number of tourists. Parking was a bit of a nightmare, and continually driving around looking for a space took the enjoyment out of the trip. To be honest Lin, I am struggling to find anything that is really a pleasure anymore, not without you.

I broke the journeys in Premiere Inns – good value! Coming home, I stopped in the Seaton one, Devon... Oh, so many memories! The tramway, the beach... you loved it there.

HOME IS BEST

When I get home on Friday, I have two weeks to get the garden into shape. Your brother and sister are coming here to see the garden on your birthday. Your oldest friend, Mandy, along with Helen and her sister Sue are invited. I will do a ploughman's snack. I will leave you to organise the good weather darling.

Last week I bit the bullet and ordered an E bike from Halfords. Got to get myself fitter! I am realising that home is best, and Rustington is quite wonderful. Every trip I take, I come home, go to the Beach bar, and the wonderful girls ask me where I have been. And I think, why did I go?

There was a Rotary day in the village last Saturday, so I popped into the church hall. Your wonderful WI ladies gave me a warm welcome.

I picked up a leaflet for the croquet club, an open day on the 7th June, and thought I might pop along. I never did though. Found out you have to wear whites... Not for me, darling!

I put a fiver in the Rotary bucket and said, "This is for Fred and Jean King, who were very involved in Hove Rotary." As you know, he was even Father Christmas on their float for many years, bless them. I do hope you are with them, and Jill, and all our other good friends who have passed.

8

WARNERS AGAIN

I am going to Cricket St Thomas with my elder brother Chris and his wife Olwyn in July. Chris expressed a wish to visit the Fleet Air Arm Museum in Yeovil. I thought it would be a good base, and Olwyn could come too. I know I'm experienced with blind people, my poor dear Blind Bongle, to use one of your pet names, but I did not know if I could cope with Chris alone for two days. This will work out well; Olwyn can tour the grounds and lake, and I get quality time with Chris at the museum for the day. It came as a bit of a shock to pay a single supplement for the first time though!

In typical Coppard 'cock-up' fashion, the damn museum does not open on a Tuesday, so we just popped in on the way home on Wednesday. But to be honest, a couple of hours there was quite enough to see it all.

On the Tuesday we went to a National Trust place, Montacute House. On the way in, I realised it was a place we had stopped before and had a night in the village pub – on the way back from a Wales trip, I think. Memories came flooding back, so I left them to explore and sat with my thoughts. I even went for a pint in that pub... Oh my, this is hard.

WOBBLING ON

St Barnabus, our local hospice, was absolutely wonderful with you, Linda, in your final weeks. You had a couple of periods in there for blood transfusions. The staff were so caring and patient, and you enjoyed me pushing you around the well-kept grounds in a wheelchair. You even remarked that you'd be ok if this was where your journey would finish. Their nurses came to our home and saw us through that horrible final period, and I cannot thank them enough.

After your ordeal was over I had regular calls to help me through those dark early days. They were a great help. When my allotted time was up, they asked if I'd like to join their bereavement craft club. I said yes, but I didn't really know what to expect.

You'd think I would dread going there, but it is such a serene, calming place and the staff are wonderful. The tutor, Steven, is a graphic designer, artist and keen photographer. I've learnt a lot over the last two years. The others in the group all draw or paint while I write; we can talk about things together that normal people would not understand, and I find it very comforting. Between the craft group and my weekly counselling call, I am starting to come to terms with grief. But by God, I miss you every waking minute.

I do think that women handle grief better. Perhaps through the ages, with men being killed in wars, hunting, and fending for the family, they developed a capacity to cope on their own. The guys opening up in the craft group make me realise that much of what I am going through is not unique to me.

The neighbours, especially Gail and Sandra, help keep me sane. We regularly go out for Sunday lunch together. I am still doing bits of shopping for the three old girls, Norma, Betty and Patricia – yes, well over two years now, but again they provide some human contact. Norma keeps me supplied with jigsaws, another sanity tool. She insists on giving me petrol money if I go away, bless her, so I bring her little treats like raspberries now and again.

It also may come as a surprise that the doctors and nurses at Westcourt Surgery have been going the extra mile to look after me since I lost you, my dearest.

The latest is, I have been referred to 'Arun Wellbeing.' A wonderful lady called Wendy phoned me back – I think they were worried I might top myself! I hope I'm over that, but thank goodness I took all your morphine back to the pharmacy... Who knows what might happen, those nights when the demons come calling?

Anyhow, I will get support to lose weight and help with alcohol. We always enjoyed our wines, but these last two years have been ridiculous. It's slowly killing me, but I can see a light; time will tell. My breathing is rubbish, but I hope the exercise bike will help.

Leap forward to October. I have found it hard to get my writing head on, but more on that shortly.

Friday, 28th October, a date I have been dreading: the anniversary of your passing. I decided it was time for the final physical act, for your ashes to become one with your beloved garden.

Your brother and sister, Sara and Ian came. My brother Bruce and Sandra from downstairs attended, too. I put your ashes in the collapsible washing up bowl we used when camping, and using the garden scoop you used in endless hours of 'mud busting', we laid you to rest. We chose the borders you could see from your seat in the summerhouse. Rest in peace, my darling.

ST BARNABAS

I have to do a bit of catching up now my dear. Some people might think it strange that I talk to you as though you are sitting next to me. To which I would say, if you have been as fortunate as we have, to find 'the one', then a part of you will always be with me, in me. Thus, we are 'one' forever.

A while ago, at St Barnabas Craft Club, Stevan, the tutor, asked us to bring in something from home that resembled ourselves, or made us think of ourselves in some light.

I choose a pair of pipe pliers. Like me, they are a funny shape, and very adaptable for a multitude of tasks. Then we were asked to create a piece of 'art' around the object.

It seemed logical to use plumbing pipes, so I made a square, adding a pipe that went up and over from one side to the other like the handle of a basket. I put a shut-off valve in the centre of that handle and added colours to different sections of the pipes to represent a flowing storyline for the different stages of our lives. I called it, 'Life Cycle'. It's now on loan to St Barnabas, where it will be featured in an art exhibition.

I said, if it ever ends up in an auction for £1 million, I will split it with them!

Here is the script I wrote to go with the sculpture:

Pink for a girl, blue for a boy; they meet, unite, and together the green
shoots of a new love appear.
Then the yellow spring of an evolving relationship, maturing into a
wonderful life together.
They reach the midlife point – the 'stopcock'! For some, divorce and separation; if lucky, the valve is open for the next, most companionable of stages.
The pliers signify the maintenance that all relationships need, to be worked at, equally.
For the lucky ones, they flow into the golden age of companionship and true
lasting love and devotion.
Inevitably there comes the separation, for one, the black of death, hopefully swift and painless. For the survivor, a grey lonely wilderness, waiting to be reunited...
And so the cycle begins again.

11

WOBBLING AGAIN

November is upon us my dear, time seems to be flying by. I am off to Ventura again on the 12th, two weeks down to the Canaries – I even got our cabin, L312! Oh, the memories. I hope that this time around I will be better placed, mentally, to enjoy it. I think the one last year in December was too early; I was still a mess. But more on Ventura as it unfolds! Your faithful Samsung tablet finally gave up the ghost, starting up and then shutting down straight away. It was so good though that I bought another one. Although cheaper, the A8 works very well and I shall be taking it with me. I have MS Word and Excel on it, so a home from home.

It never ceases to amaze me how memories can suddenly leap out at you unexpectedly. Take last night, watching Top Gear. The lads were driving super cars around Germany, this time to compare 'enjoyment levels' instead of speed and handling. It made a nice change. They drove through Rosenheim, and stopped for a stein of lemonade and a sausage. *Bratwurst mit brot!* My, how you loved your sausage shacks!

Rosenheim was the nearest large town to Prien am Chiemsee, one of our all time favourite places: Herr Wolf's hotel, the 'Leopold', next to the dockside. More on that later.

Now back to Top Gear. The team moved into Austria and headed for the Grossglockner mountain pass, the road that goes all the way through to the Italian Tirol. I think they had the road to themselves, and the cars loved it. It was described as one of the world's best and most scenic drives.

My darling, we have driven that road three or four times over the years and it is a truly wonderful experience. I think the first time was in the hired blue VW Golf that we christened Willie, from the number plate. We went all the way up to the glacier; I think that trip was a bit grey and gloomy. Then again, on the holiday where your mother, Jean, came along. We had an Avis hire car – a Mercedes A Class. She was astounded at the views; that trip was sunny, I think. Then another Mercedes, a B class this time which we loved. On the way up we saw a marmot by the road – you were terrified it would run out in front of us! As we reached higher altitudes we came across snow; at some points it was higher than the car! We took the freshly-ploughed Alpine road to the glacier and the numerous viewpoints and restaurants. But the most fun was on our road trip in our own Seat Altea Sport. That was a great experience; the power and sport suspension made it an exhilarating drive. Now, my dearest, it is all about remembering the good times, of which there are many, thank goodness. There are so many more tales from Austria and Bavaria still to tell, we really were very lucky in many ways.

12

THE PERSONAL STUFF

As I mentioned earlier, I have been giving a lot of thought as to how to write this book. It's a wonderful way of capturing memories, some of which are long forgotten. I am instinctively writing in a style which is just as though we are sitting in the summerhouse, chatting on a peaceful Sunday afternoon. Elaine Paige is on the radio, a bottle of Marlborough Sauvignon Blanc sits on the table between us in that lovely *Le Creuset* cooling sleeve we bought in France. I need to know if it works before going too far.

I have sent the first six or so pages to your childhood girlfriends for some feedback. I am pleased to say they absolutely loved it, and are telling me they want more. Encouragement enough to continue! I also feel it is quite therapeutic... Oh my darling, I still miss you so much.

Now, before I go any further, I must raise the subject of our 'silly words' and nicknames, so I can use them here (as is apt) without confusing our dear readers.

Me first, as you never really gave me a nickname – just 'Stevie Pete' on occasion, or 'Mr Grumpy', my jokey nickname from our days at EDF Energy. But you, my dear, had an ever-evolving series of names. I suppose the ideas began with odd things your family used to say. 'Sheepies' for sheep, 'Glick Glocks' for horses, and 'Made up' for when you were really pleased with something. But you, my dear Linda, started out being called 'Bonkie' by me. Obvious naughty connotations may have existed in our early years, but it was really due to your lack of peripheral vision. If you tried to look at the view while walking you had no idea what was directly in your path and often 'bonked' into them! Bollards and toddlers beware!

Back then you had not been trained to use a long cane, hell you were even still driving, Lord help us! 'Bonkie' then softened into 'Bongle', or even 'Bingle Bongle', a much more cosy and comforting name. Blimey, they'll think we're mad! We also had daft words for situations, if something was really nice we would call it 'Chumbley' – meaning comforting, cosy. And then there is 'Wobble'. Wobble was the word we used to attract each other's attention, particularly in a crowd; it also came to mean an experience, hence its use here as some chapter headings. But my dearest Bongle, the crowning star of your nicknames has to be 'Bonkie the Intrepid'. This title you so richly deserved at times of exploration! You would let me lead you on rocky paths to waterfalls, around lakes and up snowy mountain tops, sometimes with two ski poles which I had covered in white tape. When we reached a summit or spectacular view point another special word would come into play; 'Gringling', when you would be so happy that you grinned from ear to ear. I am overjoyed that most of our photos show you gringling away, and it makes me so happy to know that you were really 'made up'. You were so damned brave considering what little you could see, but when we reached our destination you would stop and slowly scan in the view, and that wonderful grin would appear on your face.

I am glad I wrote this bit in my cabin, tears are rolling down my face. Oh god, I miss you, Bongle. Oh! How could I forget the most important and truly fantastic word: 'SQUABBLE!' Yes, it should be in capitals: SQUABBLE! Our merging of a wonderful hug combined with a cuddle. At the mention of this word we would leap up and embrace each other in a show of love. Oh, what I would not give for a squabble now, my beautiful Bongle.

13

TWO CLOTS IN A CAMPER

Now, I am in a bit of a quandary about what to do with *Two Clots in a Camper,* the book I wrote and published about our very first grand tour of France, Spain and Portugal. The trip and the book played a big part in our early lives, and in your last few months. After you tragically lost the little bit of sight you had, from the brain tumours, damn them, it was hard to know how to amuse you. You had even lost interest in your talking books, I cannot imagine the personal hell you were going through. I was so busy and exhausted trying to look after you, I wonder even now if I could have done more to ease your torment. But I do know you loved me reading to you, bits from the Mail on Sunday, especially Mindy Hammond's column. I would read you a chapter at a time from *Two Clots,* and we would savour the stories and the memories from way back in 1994. We were time-travellers for a short while, back in our youthful bodies on an exciting journey through lands with borders and currencies, culinary treats and many adventures.

It was 1994. You were given redundancy notice from your long-term job with the Alliance Building Society; they were merging with the Leicester Society, no way did we want to move up there! So you opted for redundancy. We figured that, after 20 years, the money would be pretty good. We had often talked – well, day-dreamed, about travelling around Europe. We started looking around for old camper vans. Long before the days of the Internet, you had to rely on local papers and things like the Friday Ad. We found our future van less than two miles away in Hove. A VW Holdsworth Villa conversion for only £1600. It was high mileage, but we were told it'd had a second-hand engine put in recently, which was 1800cc instead of the standard 1600. I was working as a self-employed mechanic, so would have a few weeks to do it up and make some improvements. We christened him (Her? It?) 'Pooh the Bus,' – not so much after Pooh Bear, but because it was a scruffy piece of poo for us to transform!

Pooh had a canvas pop-top rising roof, a two burner hob and grill, a small 'rock and roll' double bed that in the day was a bench seat. A cupboard with the essential (well, to me) Porta-potty, a wardrobe and plenty of cupboard space. The sink was fed from a five-gallon water bottle under the bed, with a rubber bulb pump on the floor by the sink. I converted this to 12 volt electric using a windscreen washer pump. We had no mains electricity or heating, but it would suffice. The standard VW slab front seats were not very comfortable, so I adapted a pair of seats from an MG Metro. They looked great! I fitted a mini roof rack above the cab to hold the canvas awning we'd been given; this would provide an outside room and greatly add to our living space. I gave the van a full service and a thorough going over. Pooh was all white, but the lower half was a bit tatty, so I re-sprayed the lower quarters bright red. Pooh was ready to roll! We had a couple of trial weekends, and were over the moon with our new home from home.

I set about planning our route while you worked out your notice. We would sit together in the evenings with a bottle of wine, going over the plans. No Internet in those days, just a large scale map book, a couple of campsite guides and one of those long-redundant pens with a little wheel in the end that would tot up distances when run along the map route.

We would go at the beginning of June, we decided. Ferry to Caen in Normandy, drive down the west coast of France, turn right along Northern Spain, head down the Atlantic coast of Portugal and into Spain. We planned to meet your mum and dad at their timeshare apartment in Benalmádena on the Costa Del Sol, in September, for a final week of luxury. What idiots! Up north in the cool early summer and down south in searing high season... We got it so wrong, but we had a mammoth adventure regardless!

We held a farewell party for family and friends, inviting them to take a tour of the van – not that a grand tour of a campervan takes more than 30 seconds! After the party we had around fifteen bottles of wine left. We must be the only people who ever took wine TO France! Two Clots indeed. We sailed from Portsmouth to Caen with an open return ticket that we could upgrade to return from a different port if need be. On this trip there was still the excitement of international borders to cross and several different currencies, an element of romance lost on travellers today.

I won't dwell on the details too much, as it's all in the book. We drove through Normandy, passing the majestic St Michael's Mount, then on to the Atlantic coast, wending our way down to the Spanish border. We opted for the new toll motorway to get close to Santander, often high up on bridges between rolling green hills, looking down on beautiful coves and villages. Sumo, just across the estuary from Santander, was our destination for a week. We found a campsite owned by an English couple, Edna and Harry, and had a fabulous time there. We got quite friendly with them, even doing odd jobs in exchange for evening beers.

We continued hopping along Spain's northern coast before turning south for Portugal's Atlantic Silver Coast. It was a fantastic adventure for us; many unspoilt village campsites, Porto Covo being a favourite, as yet untouched by mass tourism. Remember all the cat food we bought to feed the strays that flocked to you at nearly every campsite? You loved it, and wanted to adopt them all, bless you.

The Algarve followed, with Praia da Luz (our first chips for two weeks!) and Lagos being highlights. You loved the seafood here, especially sardines. At a beach hut with a charcoal barbecue, we gave the old boy a few *escudos* in return for a plate, a chunk of bread and a cold beer. Outside, his son placed five sizzling silver sardines on our plates, delicious! We sat on the beach watching the locals walking in the sand. They seemed to be sifting the wet sand with their feet, then bending down to pick up something. We later saw a couple boil a saucepan on a camping burner, and proceeding to cook the clams or cockles, before eating them with rustic bread!

Spain and the Costa Del Sol was next on our route, the rugged west coast around Cadiz and Jerez, then up in the hills overlooking Gibraltar and the Atlas Mountains of North Africa. As it was a Sunday, I thought it wise to fill up the van, not knowing what might be open in the British outpost. Sadly, the garages were, and much cheaper than Spain! You just sighed. I do wonder how often you let me take the lead, just for a quiet life? We did enjoy a full English breakfast though, and explored the place, but the likes of Marks and Spencer were closed, much to your annoyance.

Estepona was our next destination, which you were really looking forward to. Unfortunately I missed the turn off, and we ended up at our next campsite near Marbella. I don't think you ever quite forgave me, but we did visit Estepona many times in later years. Then we meandered east, stopping where the fancy took us. It was getting hotter and hotter, and living in a tin box was getting to be quite unpleasant at times. It was then that I learned of a job offer back home, after phoning my mother. We decided to cut our adventure short and travel home over the next two weeks. We settled on a final three nights of luxury in the beautiful town of Nerja. The Hostel Marazul was our air-conditioned haven for that wonderful time. We found a little cove with huge rocks that we sat in front of on tiny pebbles, our feet just inches from the water. Lilo Lil had an outing, as we relaxed in the blissfully calm waters, warm enough even for you, my darling. In the evening we found a little Brit bar on the way to the Old Town. We chatted to the owner, Dave, and had a pre-dinner beer. In the Old Town some restaurants had tables set up in the car-free street. We had your long-awaited Pil Pil prawns, sizzling in Tapas bowls straight from the oven. You were in seventh heaven, with more fish to follow.

It soon became time to hit the road north. We decided to head back to Sumo and get the Brittany ferry from Santander to Portsmouth for a last bit of luxury. It was to be a tedious two-day drive straight up through the centre of Spain, but the old Pooh Bus had done us proud and we were sure she would get us home. You must remember how hot and damn boring that journey was; endless olive groves stretching for mile after mile across the plain. We finally made it back to Sumo to find the campsite surprisingly full. Then we found out why: the ferry was not being allowed into port by the blockading French fishermen! Damn them, they are always up in arms about something.

We gave it a couple of days and then decided to hot foot it to Caen. So much for our luxury trip home! Back in Caen two days later we made the ferry – just. Remember, they said we were too late, but when we told them we'd driven from Santander they held the ship up and even gave us a cabin for free. We went on deck and shared a table to watch our departure over a final French beer. A gentleman asked if we'd seen that little red and white campervan that came late, and the crew reopened the doors for. "Must be VIPs," he said. We laughed and told him our tale. Our Grand Tour was over, my darling, but what an adventure, and so many memories made.

14

CANARIES CRUISE

Well my dear, here I am again on Ventura. I'm off to the Canaries, not one we've done before, for two whole weeks. The first day was a mix of highs and lows. Your white cane always made the boarding formalities a breeze, fast track all the way – a small advantage of your disability, my darling Bongle.

Of course I hit the casino, actually made £175 on the roulette! It would be nice to keep that up... well, we'll see. I've only eaten in the buffet so far, same as always.

Last night I was rudely awakened at 2.30am and told to get up and go downstairs. A helicopter was coming in to pick up a medical emergency. With us being on the top deck, we all had to evacuate – only they didn't say where to! I met a couple and we wandered around aimlessly, with nothing open and no-one else in sight. Eventually we got the all clear at 3.45 am. Another minor niggle; there's a leak from the sink waste pipe. At first I thought it was just me being messy! I'm waiting for a plumber now... Ho hum, nothing is ever plain sailing, eh! Airies the steward is nice, though. He changed the beds to singles for me last night, so more space and a more manageable quilt.

Our first stop is Lisbon. We loved it, until you fell and did your ankle in. You were in agony and had to wear that ruddy moon boot for a month. Then it will be Cadiz, another favourite of ours... I don't know if I'll be going ashore or not, I'll decide on the day. I had to get out of the cabin as the plumber came, so I've spent a lazy afternoon reading. Now it's time for the first bingo session... I won't hold my breath.

Now, do you recall that lovely cruise around the Mediterranean, and our day trip to Pisa? The guide went haring off and we adopted that old dear who couldn't keep up. We missed the guided tour and did our own thing... I always was a soft touch. It was a stunning place, though. You did the compulsory thing and held up the tower while I snapped you. The old lady was a smoker, too, and kept stopping to light up... I can't believe I was so patient with her. Then there was your favourite sail away, Gibraltar. There was a sister ship alongside, her sirens blasting – Oceana I think. You were singing away in the sunshine, waving your Union Jack flags. I snuck off for a lovely dip in the deserted health club pool, then joined you for a drink. It was wonderful!

As for this cruise... I should be grateful, but I just cannot find any pleasure. Even the casino is becoming a bore. I broke even last night, but being me, went back later and lost it! I won the first line at bingo and had to share it three ways, but at least it paid for the tickets.

I tried to be good this morning and went to the gym at 7.45. It was packed. I am so self-conscious of this hernia that I did five minutes on a bike and then went for a walk. I looked in the mirror last night – never a good thing – and decided that if I got a marker pen and did two dots for nostrils and two little piggy eyes, my lump would look like a pig's head erupting from my tummy! I have a meeting at the gym when I get home. I've got to take it seriously now, it's beyond a joke.

I fear I have become one of 'the lost boys'. You see us dotted around the ship, obviously widowers, sitting alone, a slightly glum, almost shell-shocked expression on our faces. Trying to recapture past memories perhaps, or desperately seeking someone to chat to. Some, like me, are content to observe. The ladies tend to travel in pairs or groups, and seem much more at ease with their situation. Well, on the surface, anyway. I do wonder if I will ever find some enjoyment again. Is a camper van the answer? A lot of money to waste if it is not. Still, that's out of the question at the moment. It's not even 10 am! What the hell am I meant to do now? At least there's a film at 11.30.

Lisbon tomorrow. It should be quiet on board, so I can do some laundry. I have so little that fits me now, I have to keep turning it around.

I think that, as I'm (I wanted to put 'we' then!) headed to the Canaries, places we enjoyed many times, it would be a good to recall those trips from the early days.

Fuerteventura, not that long after we married; Caleta de Fuste, a package trip. We had a brand new little apartment on a complex about ten minutes' walk from town, with a nice pool and a clubhouse. We were skint in those days, so we found a chicken and chips takeaway near the beach. We had that most nights, and then we walked to that dingy little nightclub and sat on cushions drinking Bacardi and coke. We got so sick of that drink, it put us off for years! We hired a little Citroën for 3 days, and I disconnected the speedo to keep the mileage down. We went all over the island! Do you remember those two beautiful Scandinavian hitchhikers we gave a lift to? They told us about a nudist beach behind a giant sand dune... We dropped them off and then went ourselves. It was full of mainly overweight Germans, but we had a wonderfully liberated swim. It was a bit weird going to the beach snack bar for lunch... we'd gone off the sausages, for some reason!

We explored the island, and walked for miles along the beaches. We found those little stones – hollow, with tiny holes in the side, they looked like monkey-nut shells. We called them fossilised camel turds. There are still a couple on the shelf in the summerhouse. One night they had bingo in the pool bar. When we won the full house, it topped up our spends so we could really enjoy the rest of our stay. Memories, my darling! That is all there is now.

Playa Blanca on Lanzarote deserves a huge mention; two wonderful timeshare resorts next to each other, only a few yards from the many restaurants, bars and the beach. There was a small harbour where the ferries sailed from. From one of our patios we could easily see them come and go. 'Big Fred' and 'Throbbie,' we called them.

I shall digress for a spell. Lisbon again, and a truly dismal day; low cloud and drizzle, but it makes my choice to stay on board a bit easier. There's too many memories here... mainly wonderful ones, except for the last time. Walking back towards Ventura, you stumbled and turned your ankle. Two hunky deckhands helped you up, but that bastard taxi driver refused to take us to the ship as it was so close. You were in agony and I was powerless to ease your pain. Should I have been studying the ground more closely? Should I have called an ambulance? I helped you hobble back, and a lovely guy bought down a wheelchair and got you to the cabin to await the medics. A month in a moon boot followed. Why, my wobbly one, was it always you that had these mishaps? As you often said, after the devastating diagnosis, "I must have been someone terrible in a past life." You, dear, sweet, kind Linda, did not deserve what life threw at you. Rest now, my darling. We will be together soon.

On board I have time to think. Too much time, really. So much has changed with your passing, daily life is completely different. I get no pleasure from food; even drinking and gambling are becoming a bore. The housework goes undone, unless someone is coming – a rarity, nowadays. I know I am in poor shape, but cannot work up any enthusiasm to change. Fitness is becoming a real issue – my breathing is awful, my mobility getting worse. I will try to do better. You wanted me to have a life, but God it's hard to think of any future without my other old sock.

Back to Playa Blanca. That huge heated swimming pool, the largest on the island at the time, with the friendly old lifeguard on hand to help you into the pool. It was so warm, you didn't need persuading to take a dip. We spent a lot of time in there. In later years more and more families came, as they inherited their parents' timeshares. I think that was partly why we gave them up – that, and the companies were swallowed up by tour operators and they rented out the nicest resorts privately. Still, if we'd kept the timeshares we might never have bought our motor home, or discovered cruising.

You recall the time Jill and Jim were staying in a hotel in Playa Blanca, not far from us? That was quite a sociable week for us. As usual we had a hire car, it always seemed to be a Skoda Fabia Estate in Lanzarote, but good enough for us. We took them out for day trips to Fire Mountain, the volcanic wasteland, the crashing sea caves and right around the island one day. Jill was always so enthusiastic about everything. I know you loved having company for lunch instead of just boring old me. They were half-board, but we met up for drinks after diner. That was a good holiday, but the damn cancer got Jill in the end. It always seems to win, evil thing that it is.

Your dear mother came with us a couple of times as well, she loved the sun and the two of you would lounge by the pool for hours... I would get bored and go for a wander. And a beer, of course!

The more I delve back into our glorious thirty-one years together, the more holidays and trips I remember. Blimey girl, we didn't half have some! Driving holidays, camping trips, villas and hotels, good and bad... can I mention them all? Or will it be too boring and repetitive? There are obvious places that need recalling, stunning Austria and Bavaria... Hey! Stop singing 'The hills are alive'! I need thinking time now, to plan what to write next. Catch you later, Lin.

We reached Cadiz today, in the grey and drizzle. I think everyone is getting a bit fed up with the weather. I just hope the Canaries are bathed in sunshine. When we were here together it was warm and sunny. We took the open top tourist bus, it was a good way to see the sights, especially for you – you could take in the view without having to look at the ground. Perhaps I should explain, in case someone reads this who does not know you. Your right eye was totally blind, the legacy of a lifetime of glaucoma, but your left eye had a small, clear window. No peripheral vision; it was like looking through a gun sight. If you weren't aiming at it, you couldn't see it; children and bollards were your worst nightmares on a walk. You needed time to 'scan in' the views.

That bus took us all around the old town, brushing palm trees as we went, along the beachfront to the ancient harbour fortress where we got off for a while. We had an ice cream on the smooth, golden sandy beach, before walking the fortress walls overlooking a sparkling blue sea. By the entrance an artist was painting beach scenes on flat pebbles. We bought one; it still sits in the summerhouse, along with all our other mementos and knick knacks, all prompts for these wonderful memories.

Do you recall the Metropolis bar on Ventura? Way up on deck eighteen, right across the back of the ship, looking down on the rear pool and the sea beyond? It was one of our favourite places; so elegant, with a pianist playing in the early evenings before dinner. Luckily, not everyone knows about it, so it can be quite peaceful. The bar doesn't open until five, so it is quiet in the day. This is where I sit writing, at the long bar under the windows, on those high chairs we always struggled into. I bring up a coffee from the buffet and sit here tapping away on my Samsung tablet. I'm afraid your expensive one gave up the ghost a couple of months ago. So here I am, writing away; before me is the working port, with enormous cranes, an endless sea of containers and the vast car park. Lots of motors homes and camper vans down there; I guess it must be free to park there, like the ports in France. I remember we said 'one day…' Sadly, now it will never be.

Another sea day, with so much time to think. I miss your guiding hand and level head. There is nobody now to curb my reckless and often rash behaviour, like my constantly changing cars. But I think the new Honda CRV auto is the one for a while. It's like driving your favourite armchair, and much less stressful in our never-ending road works and traffic jams. I'm missing it already, and the beach bar and their welcoming staff… Silly isn't it! Most people would give an arm to be on Ventura, but I would happily pop home for a day.

Gazing down from my lofty perch, the sun has decided to show itself at last. Couples lie below and around the rear pool, mostly our age, many asleep, a few holding hands. It makes the pain of what was snatched away from us even harder to bear. I don't have a clue what might give me some peace or pleasure in the future, but I'm starting to think it's not travel or cruises. Not alone. And let's be honest, most people realise what a prat I am after five minutes! It took years for us to truly understand each other. That won't happen again.

Now, 'onwards and upwards,' as Mr Wilson (one of my nicer managers at EDF Energy) used to say. Nicer, because he also used to say, 'you do what you have to do.' And I did, and travelled widely to do it too. Data Management that was… 'Nuff said.

15

THE 'H' WORD

There comes a point in this tale of our adventures that the 'H' word must come out: Hastings and Grace's Wine Bar. Thankfully, there needs to be a bit of scene setting before we get on to that nightmarish year; it can't all be jolly memories, but we did endure it together.

A while before our first great adventure, touring Europe in Pooh Bus campervan, I'd gone for an interview as a mechanic at the Brighton Territorial Army base. I had some experience on Land Rovers, so thought I might have a chance at a steady job for a change. No dice; Captain Donald, the Commanding Officer, chose an ex-army man instead. So off we went, with no plans or time limits, our budget being the only constraint. Perhaps we would find work, or our own little bit of paradise?

Around the tenth week away, I called home to see how my mother was. She said Captain Donald had been in touch, and there was a job if I wanted it. Linda, you were so eager to see me gainfully employed at last, and shouted 'Yes!'. So we headed home, but it was by no means an easy journey from the Costa del Sol. That tale is in 'Two Clots in a Camper', so I won't repeat it here.

I loved that job. I was a civil servant, with good money, good workmates and a nice pension. The only real requirement was to be able to drink copious amounts of tea in the seemingly endless procession of tea breaks. They also put me through my HGV test so I could drive the big rigs we had on the base – even the thirty-two-geared Scammel breakdown monster truck! Linda, you had a job with the Legal Aid Board, but with a far stricter regime. You used to call me jammy, but you were pleased that I was happy. It must have been around 1998, and we were missing our campervan when I found out that the Air Cadets had a Renault Master minibus with a broken camshaft. It had been sitting in a hanger for months. I thought, 'what a camper that would make!'. And after a donation to their funds, it was ours.

I did all the work myself, found second-hand parts, and after much towing around the base by a 4-ton army truck, Benny the Bus roared back to life. You came with me on a Saturday and we stripped out all the seats. It left us a huge space to play with. We went for a little test drive, up Dyke Road towards the Downs. This was the first time the engine had really warmed up; the 'Red X' I'd put in the bores to free up any sticking piston rings stared to burn off... We passed a Lycra-clad cyclist and engulfed him in a cloud of white smoke! Whoops...

Over the coming weeks, I crafted the interior from timber and pine cladding. Behind my seat I built a toilet compartment with a camping toilet, a wardrobe, and cupboards galore. I put two single beds in the rear above the wheel arches, with storage beneath and slats that spanned the gap to make a double. There was a mains electric hook up and even a field cooker with oven, grill and hob. This was donated by my TA friends, with strict instructions to have the side door open when cooking. We ordered bed cushions online, and you sewed the covers and curtains.

About this time, Tony Blair got in power and started to cut back on the armed forces. 'Drawdown' they called it, damn him. All our vehicles were to go to other bases for a while. We civvies were put on 'gardening leave' – we had to come in, but had no work to do. I found an empty hanger, dragged in a compressor and set about re-spraying Benny the Bus. She was mainly white already, so I freshened up the paintwork with a blow over and added a wide maroon stripe down both sides. And with that, she was ready to roll!

We tried a weekend away in the Wye Valley, at civil service association campsite (another perk!). We drove up to the car park for Simmonds Yat, explored for a bit, saw the views, and noticed the clouds coming in. Back in Benny, feeling rather smug with a bacon sandwich and a coffee, we watched the heavens open and the tourists scurry back to their cars.

I had holiday to use up before redundancy kicked in, so off we set for a jaunt along the Loire Valley. It was glorious, and Benny never put a foot wrong. We found a wonderful site on an island in the river, looking out over the château at Saumur. We sat there for many an hour, a glass of local white wine in hand, taking in the view. It was a super trip.

We also started going away for weekends to the White Dog Inn, set on a hill overlooking Bodiam Castle in East Sussex. There were a handful of camping pitches next to the pub, which included use of the owners private swimming pool. Over dinner one night (our favourite, plaice stuffed with prawns), I said those fateful words to the landlord. "This place is perfect. If I ever win the lottery, I'd buy it in a heartbeat." If only I'd known...

The next day, over a lunchtime drink, the landlord approached us. "Did you mean that, last night? Have you had any experience in the licensed trade?"

"Yes," I said, "I've been a bar cellar man a few times, and back when I was twenty-one I managed a night-cum-motor-yacht-club near Brighton."

"Well," he said, "I've just bought a pub in Hastings, and I want to turn it into a wine bar..."

We were hooked!

That Sunday lunchtime we went for a look at Grace's Wine Bar. It was on a corner between the station and the Priory Meadow shopping centre, with the British Legion club adjacent. It looked quite nice; there was a pretty blonde lady behind the bar, a long-haired man reading the paper, a group of blokes in the little pool room and a few people sitting at the tables, having a drink. None of it was wine, though! It was nicely decorated, but really still a pub (apart from a wine rack at the end of the bar). We didn't make ourselves known, just had a drink and chatted. If only we'd visited on a Saturday night, instead...

We told our potential new boss that we were interested. He said he would take us down for a full look around in the morning, and introduce us to the current landlady, who wanted to leave. In short, we accepted. We had to go on licensee and food hygiene courses, and be ready to move in in eight weeks! Wow!

There was a couple who were trying to buy up all the flats in our block. They offered to be our letting agents; if things worked out in Hastings, they could then buy our flat. I'm not sure I should say 'ours,' as it was all yours before I came along. In those days I hadn't fully proved my worth! They found us a tenant, a middle aged college tutor… she sounded fine, so that was that.

We took Benny up to a certain street near Wimbledon where youngsters on their gap year go to grab a campervan bargain. Of course, they all wanted VW surf buses, but a middle aged couple from New Zealand looked Benny over and fell in love with the space. Sold! £2000 in our hands and a train home. I was a bit sad; there was a lot of 'us' in Benny the Bus. They sent emails for a while from all over Europe, Benny doing them proud… they even talked of transporting Benny back home to New Zealand. I'd like to think so.

So we moved house and got to work running the pub. That's what all the customers wanted it to be! But it soon became obvious that all was not as it seemed. The blonde landlady had fallen out with the owner; she used to be one of his barmaids at the country pub, until he set her up in Grace's. Ulterior motives? I won't comment on that. On the surface she was nice to us during the transition, but the regulars were under the impression it was our fault she was leaving. Things turned nasty; the pool team, a gang of builders, and fans of the attractive landlady, took instant dislike to us – to the point of offering to redecorate the place with pick axe handles! There were six of them, including the long-haired guy, Dave, from that first Sunday visit. One of them, tall and gangly, was called 'Nutty' – probably because he had 'Nutty' tattooed on his forehead!

There were often bands on a Saturday and we stayed open till 1 am. It was hell, but we were fortunate with our staff… Although, a year after we escaped, one of them was convicted of murder! And we used to let him sleep in our lounge if he worked on Saturday! Plus we found signs of people doing drugs in the toilets, and were certain that a few were dealing... Definitely not the Hastings we'd imagined!

We closed on Mondays and Tuesdays, which was very welcome. We often drove home to see our folks. The owner wanted us to get a food operation going for bar snacks and something in the first-floor dining room. I decided on a Tapas-style menu and even got a butcher to make us Spanish chorizo sausages! Had we been in the main part of town it might have worked, but sadly, like the wine bar idea, it was a dead duck.

We slowly started winning over the pool team. Well, you really, my darling. You were like a surrogate mother to them. 'Mrs Pub', we all called you. I even started playing pool with them. Dave was in everyday, he and his partner lived nearby. We got very friendly with them, and often spent Sunday lock-in playing pool in the afternoons, after we closed at 3pm.

About this time, our so called 'lady' tenant moved her reprobate nephew in and stopped paying the rent. Neighbours told us of noisy parties and drugs, and our agents were powerless to get them out. The pool team did offer to go down and evict them though, such was the effect you had on them, my dear!

The weekends were a steady trade, but in the week it was appalling. Some days we'd only take £20. The owner had really got it wrong with this place. Some nights we would be in the bar all evening on our own, and thinking of shutting up at 9.30, when in would come George for his bloody half of Guinness!

There was another old boy who would pop in for a last pint after his regular pub crawl. After a few drinks he gained a bit of a stutter. One night he came in dripping wet and even more filthy than usual. When he ordered his pint, I said, "Shouldn't you go home and dry off?" He said, "Not yet, after my pint! I was crossing the park to get here, and I tripped on that little fence and fell into the pond!"

We'd had enough and wanted to leave, but the owner asked us to hang on while he found a buyer. He offered us a bonus, so reluctantly we accepted. Meanwhile, we started eviction proceedings against our tenant, put a deposit down on a nice VW Komet campervan, and started planning our second grand tour.

In the spring of 2000 we were finally free. We moved our stuff into storage at Hove and set off in the van, while the eviction was still going through. We retraced our previous tour to France, Spain and Portugal, we were so happy to be away from the pub that we never really thought of any new destinations. In hindsight, Germany, Austria and Italy would have been a much better choice.

16

HOVE AGAIN, NATURALLY!

Eventually, we got the flat back. I had to break in, as they never left the keys. The place was filthy, we found needles in the dining room, stuck in our once beautiful carpet. The place felt violated, and the surrounding area was changing, and not for the better. We told our letting agents to make us an offer, and to be fair they gave us a good price. Perhaps they felt a little guilty? So we set the wheels in motion. It would take a while, and we had to find another place to live, but it was all agreed on and nobody was in a rush.

You, my dear, got a job at Seaboard, the local electricity supplier, just along the road from the flat. I worked as a mechanic in Brighton. I soon got fed up with being dirty again and was envious of your nice office job. You said to me, "Why not apply?" So I did.

I attended the interview. It went OK; there were a bunch of us, and we each had to write a letter on the computer. I'd only ever used a typewriter... it was fine, until I got to the end of a line and asked where the lever was to move down the page! They all laughed so hard! And that was my introduction to wrap-around text.

Surprising us both, I got the job. It was lovely, we could walk to work and even have lunch together. The three-month training started, but after two days myself and another lady around my age were pulled out of the class. They said that, as we didn't have much experience on computers, we'd be in the back office. I had a very helpful manager, you remember Lin? That hunky ex-fireman that all the ladies fancied. He booked me onto every computer training course going, at a specialist place in Burgess Hill. I did Word, Excel, Access and Power Point, and going up the levels I loved it, especially the spreadsheets.

Now computer literate on multiple programs, I learned about the complex system of Industry Dataflow, and the little errors that happen a thousand times a day. I became a specialist, travelling all over the country and training team managers to avoid these errors. I earned access to go into the back-end of our flawed system and correct data strings that the so-called specialist programmers had installed. I think you were very proud of me, and perhaps a little surprised. Of course, you always loved the customer-facing side of business, and being with you all day was wonderful.

I can't leave the story of Seaboard like this. Re-branded EDF (for the new owners, Électricité de France), it had been so good to us, and set us up for early retirement in 2016, when your sight deteriorated even further. But thank God we did! At least we got five glorious years in, before that evil cancer took you.

We both worked in the Hove office, but they also had a smaller site in Worthing. My department was moving there, and as we now had a bungalow in Lancing, this was an easier commute. I'd become a bit of a specialist by then, so my boss had you seconded into our section and off we went. It was a lot more relaxed there. After a while you joined the small business section, as you enjoyed talking to customers. You had some wonderful managers, but then everybody loved you! You never had a bad word for anyone, and was always first-in-line to mother the youngsters. You loved it when the lads had been training in the gym, you would ask to feel their muscles as you couldn't see... They always obliged! Me, I was just known as Mr Grumpy – in an amicable way, even now I am still 'Grumps' to my old boss Carole (or 'Babes' as I used to call her).

The big boss of the company, French of course, liked getting official awards and plaques, so he asked for a Disability and Carers Network to be set up. We went to the first meeting and joined the steering committee. The chairwoman promptly went long-term sick, and we ended up building and running the thing.

We went all over the country, inspecting sites for disabled access and facilities, even Hinkley Point Nuclear power station. We created a monthly newsletter, were often hobnobbing with the really senior managers, and went to their palatial offices in London. We were on a roll. When the 2012 Olympics came, EDF was a major sponsor, and we enjoyed all the perks – like borrowing an electric Mini on the weekends, to test them in advance of the games. We had tickets for the diving (where Tom Daily gave a disappointing performance), plus two flights on the London Eye, with Champagne and canapés! The customer services director couldn't make it to the Paralympics closing ceremony, so he sent us his tickets for that, too! We were a formidable team my dear. Which makes it all the harder to be a sad old single now.

We're in Las Palmas as I write, an island we never got to visit. It looks very lush and scenic, with the sun peeping out now and then. Madeira, our favourite, is tomorrow, followed by three sea days to get home. I will be pleased to get there.

17

CARRY ON CRUISING

Madeira today. The sun is shining, and my 15th floor balcony looks straight out onto Funchal, and all the wonderful places we've strolled around on our three trips here. On our first trip, your old friend Libby was a senior manager for GB Airways, the tourist side of British Airways. She booked us those extra legroom seats directly behind Club class. We had a half-seat in between us, a real luxury to us. As we circled to land, taking in the stunning scenery, we noticed the runway poking out over the Atlantic on concrete stilts – it was a bit like landing on an aircraft carrier!

We collected our hire car and headed for Funchal. We couldn't believe how beautiful it was, bougainvillea exploding everywhere with pink, red and white blossoms. It grew like ivy, covering the concrete walls beside the roads and underpasses. Bird of Paradise plants abounded, and as we crossed towering bridges and traversed rock tunnels, I found it hard to keep my eyes on the road. We stayed in several Pestana luxury resort hotels, which incorporated a number of timeshare apartments. Pestana Palms was the first, just to the west of the famous Reid's Palace Hotel. There was a round tower block of studio apartments built right on the foreshore next to the pool; it seemed to be full of German tourists. We had a one-bedroom apartment in the gardens, directly overlooking the sea. At that time it was the most luxurious place we'd ever stayed in. There was a terrace bar in the colonial-style building, where we would sit with a vodka and tonic in the late afternoon, watching the tourist pirate galleon on its return journey. I can see it now from where I'm sitting, still moored here after all this time.

We wandered Funchal, exploring the ancient sea fort and ambling around the old town sights. We discovered the superb local snack, the 'Prego' – a round roll with an unusual texture, that was filled with hot slices of beef. Delicious! We took the cable car from the promenade, soaring up over the old town to the exotic gardens that tumble back down the mountain. We paused, hand in hand, to watch tourists clamber into wicker sledges and be pushed off down the steep road, guided by two men who steered with their special old-tyre-soled shoes. Not for us, we declared, and wandered back down through the gardens, past ponds and waterfalls, surrounded by flowers of every hue.

Another visit saw us in the Pestana Grand, a brand new hotel a little further to the west. There was direct access to the promenade, and unlike the flat strolls of the Costa del Sol, this walkway undulated with the coastline, with stairs and slopes every few hundred yards. A huge *lido* swimming centre, its pools hewn from the rock and filled with clear Atlantic sea water, looked very enticing. And there were plenty of places for a cool drink along the way – and, of course, a Prego!

We went for scenic drives to the north and to the far side of the island, navigating tunnels up to ten kilometres long, carved straight through the heart of the mountains to link various towns and villages. Before this, the roads had to skirt around the mountains, meaning long routes prone to regular rock falls. We saw some very beautiful locations and even some of the tiny traditional Madeiran wooden houses. We drove up to the Valley of Eagles and marvelled at the views; that road was not for the faint-hearted, especially with a coach coming at you around a hairpin bend!

Behind the hotel was a traditional restaurant, with a very charismatic owner. They specialised in dishes served on smouldering lava rocks, the meat smoking and still cooking in front of you, allowing you to choose how well done it was. They also did those kebabs that hang vertically from a frame, 'Donkey Dongs' we used to call them. You, of course, loved the fish; there was a speciality from Madeira's deep waters, *Espada* with banana, or 'Scabbard fish'. I'd seen them raw in the supermarkets – ugly little blighters, so it was steak for me! When it was your birthday there, they bought out a little cake and sang to you. You were 'made up,' as you often used to say. I may try and go back one day. It's a wonderful place. Thank-you, my darling Bongle, for the memories.

Well, dearest we are finally heading home. Three sea days to come, and for the first time this trip I am not wishing that you were here with me. To say we're rocking and rolling is an understatement. Everyone is tottering around like drunks – just typing this is a bit of a challenge. We're heading into a storm tonight, the captain says there will be seven-metre waves! That should be fun, so I'll batten down the hatches.

18

OUR BUNGIE

Our second home together was a bungalow in Lancing, one road back from the main coast-road and a ten-minute stroll to the beach. We could just afford it, because it was on an un-adopted estate. We loved it; a large front garden with off-street parking, a huge shed (or 'man cave') for me, and a triangular-shaped back garden with a small pond. A bonus was that we were located opposite the end of Shoreham airport runway, so we were never short of guests on air show days. We saw the Avro Vulcan 400-feet above our rooftop; the noise was so thunderous, it shook the house. We saw Harriers dance just beyond our pond, Spitfires, Hurricanes, and all types of aircraft performing as if just for us. The place was a bit of a fixer-upper, but working together with all my power tools we soon knocked it into shape. The bedroom was overlooking the rear garden, but we turned that into the lounge and built a conservatory across the back. There were sliding double doors, and we bought a nice set of wicker garden furniture. It became our favourite place. Our mothers adored it too, and often visited. It was also only a ten-minute drive to our offices in Worthing. The only downside was the non-existent pavements and the pot-holed road, parts of which flooded frequently. It was these treacherous pavements, and the threat of a huge housing development directly behind us, that made us move again in 2013.

We found a buyer for the bungalow, and toyed with the idea of renting a place and going abroad for a while. Your regular eye hospital appointments were a bit of an obstacle, but Moorfields had saved your little bit of sight many times.

One day you asked me, "Just exactly how much money have we got?" By then I was looking after all of our accounts on an Excel spreadsheet. Your sight made it hard for you to use the computer at home; at work they'd given you all sorts of aids and magnification programmes. We worked out that we might be able to afford a flat or a small property, and be mortgage free, so we started hunting.

19

RUSTIES IN RUSTINGTON

West Worthing and beyond was cheaper, and still easy to get to work from. We looked at a few places and then visited The Grangeway in Rustington. You instantly fell in love with the pavements! Shiny black asphalt, smooth, pot hole free and easy for you to navigate. The place we were viewing was one road back from the high street. Doctors, dentist, hairdressers and The Lamb pub were a short stroll away, with the wonderful seafront just a ten minute walk. And we hadn't even looked inside yet!

There was off-road parking and a concrete garage with an up-and-over door, behind which was a huge, if neglected garden twenty fence panels long and about thirty feet wide. Wow. The property was adjacent to the garden, purpose built maisonettes; we were looking at one upstairs. Maisy, we would come to call it. This was a real project; a 1950s kitchen and bathroom, but it did have modern windows and nearly new carpets throughout... It was love at first sight. We put in an offer straightaway.

In May, we took some holiday and moved in. The lounge and bedroom were habitable after a good clean, but there was lots of junk stored in the garage. We hired a skip and gutted the kitchen and bathroom. We then had to wait for the plasterers to chisel off the original tiles from both rooms; they were cemented in place, and a nightmare to remove. For two weeks, we ate in the Lamb every night. Luckily, there were showers at work, or up at your mum's house on the weekends. That renovation was a labour of love. We put in a Wickes kitchen with ceramic hob, a double oven and a twin-drainer sink. We got all new appliances, washing machine, dishwasher, tumble dryer and a fridge that had to live on the landing as the kitchen was so small. We put in a new bathroom, with a quadrant corner shower that was easy for you to use. The bathroom was also compact, so I had the brainwave of angling the toilet into the room on a flexible coupling, giving us more knee-room. A vanity unit and electric towel rail completed the space. We were comfortable and cosy.

The garden was another project. Overrun with weeds and ground ivy, it took us weeks and many visits to the tip to clear. You would sit for hours mud-busting; I would tip trug baskets full of weed-infested soil into the wheel barrow, where you would sift and sort it so it could go back into the borders. Eventually it all came together, and was our pride and joy, drawing many complimentary comments from visitors. On retiring, we built a decking platform behind the garage. You wanted a summerhouse in memory of your dear mother. I wanted to build one, but you wanted to buy one, so of course, we did. Only, it was too low and had plastic windows, so I got my project by raising it six inches and adding large glass windows. I also put in electrics so we could have light and heat, and of course another Alexa so you could control the radio. We loved it, and many a bottle of wine was enjoyed, watching the garden grow and planning the next season or holiday. We were really happy in our little Maisy the Maisonette. Of course, good neighbours help, and ours are lovely, as are the older ladies dotted around the end of our cul-de-sac. I live there still.

20

BACK TO THE TRAVELS

I think we're about due to return to our wonderful travel adventures. But which ones, out of so many? France, Austria, Germany? Well, we only stayed in Italy once, so let's begin with that – and that horrible little Vauxhall hire car with the electric handbrake. What year was it? This is where your photographic memory for dates, places, names (and my misdemeanours) would be handy, Bongle!

But first, that really was a night of rocking and rolling, and it's getting rougher all the time. We'll be entering the Bay of Biscay anytime, notorious for its bumpy passage. It's comical, watching people walk with the sway of the ship; I just saw an elderly lady taking small steps and waddling along, she looked like a penguin!

It's supposed to be Black Tie again tonight, if they don't cancel it. I suspect some of the stage shows will not go forward. I can't dress up, my long-sleeved shirts for ties no longer adequately cover my growing umbilical hernia. It's gross, and a cause for concern. I will just come up here at 5.30pm for an hour, before the dress code kicks in. Kyra the

Warrior Princess might be joining me for a drink, if she has time... Intrigued?

One of the acts on board is a guitar playing busker called Sinead Hayes. She's about thirty, attractive, with bright red hair and she wears red platform shoes. Tony James Slater, my author friend in Australia, writes humorous travel books, but under the pen name 'Tyler Aston' he's written several sci-fi books. Five are in the 'Earth Warden' series, I have just read books four and five whilst on board. One of the lead characters is Kyra, the Warrior Princess; one of her talents is the ability to change her hair colour at will, from her regular rainbow to bright red for battle. She also has a passion for earth shoes, particularly red. To complete the scene, Kyra is aged around 100, but equates to 30 earth years. So when I saw Sinead on stage I had to message Tony and say. "I think your Kyra has a side-line!" Now, this is where it all gets a bit weird... Tony asked me to get a picture! Oh, blimey. I saw her again later on, in the crew section of the buffet, having lunch. She could think I'm a pervy old stalker and tell me to get lost, I thought... but here goes! I begged her pardon for the interruption and told my tale. She was charming – and slightly bemused – but she let me take a picture for Tony.

Later, after watching her play her set in the bar, I said, "If you have time for a drink before we get home, I'll tell you about your alter ego, Kyra." And I gave her a note with the book's info on Amazon, and Tony's name, so she wouldn't think I was mad. I told her that I go to the Metropolis bar at 5.30 every afternoon, and to her credit she said, "I'll try to get up there." So, there's two more nights left to see if she makes it. Oh, Tony's comment on the photo was, "Wow, she's gorgeous!" Yes mate, she is. Surreal or what? Oh wait! My friendly barman, Rickson, who knows this tale, tells me she came up here last night asking for me, about two minutes after I left!

It was Black Tie again last night. I think that's something that should be replaced with 'smart dress' – it's only slim men who look good in formal eveningwear, unless you can afford Pavarotti's tailor! I just look like a heap. Ladies can get away with floaty dresses, but us fat boys look ridiculous. Last night I wore a nice shirt under my linen jacket, but despite being a regular customer I was asked to leave or get a tie! I knew it would happen, but I was testing them a bit. Shame they don't enforce the 'smart casual' dress code on the oinks who wear shorts and sleeveless shirts in the other venues! Yuk.

21

ITALY

Italy. I'd been trying to get us into this timeshare resort for years; a very popular mountain hotel, with only a handful of timeshare apartments. I finally bagged us a one-bedroom spot in June, one of our usual traveling periods with our anniversary on the 2nd and your birthday on the 8th. We flew into our favourite airport, small and friendly Salzburg in Austria. We always booked a Group B hire car with Avis, and in Austria we'd been rewarded with an Audi S line, Mercedes B class, Skoda Yeti and even a Jeep... So imagine my horror when handed the keys to a Vauxhall Astra! It was the same time as the famous Passion Play just over the border in Bavaria, so all the larger cars were booked. We collected the Astra and I got in. There was no handbrake lever, which was unheard of back then; eventually I found a switch near the gear lever. It was either on or off, no hill start assist like now. This was going to be tricky on the mountain roads. I instantly hated that car. It was a boring little white thing, and gutless when pulling off. I was so disappointed, as I loved driving a nice car on holiday. The only consolation was that we could swap it for a Mercedes when we moved back for our second week in Austria. Not a good start.

The hotel was wonderful, stone-built with a large courtyard to the rear where sumptuous buffet dinners were served. it overlooked a large pool surrounded by timber decking and covered with sunbeds. The views over the pine-clad mountainside were stunning. It was so quiet and peaceful, too. Our apartment was beautifully appointed, with the same great views from our balcony. I said to you that it was worth waiting for to get in there; you said that it was a shame we weren't allowed to come again for three years, as per the timeshare rules. But we were here now, and it was gorgeous. There was even a heated indoor pool and Jacuzzi – perfect!

The village was really just a cluster of houses, but there was a stream running through it that used to power a small water mill. One stretch was covered in, with stone pools where villagers used to do their laundry and bathing... I think 'quaint' is the word. We found it was very tranquil, and quite lovely. The nearby small town of Lana had a Lidl, where we bought copious amounts of a crisp, lemony white Soave and a few nibbles for the room. One day we drove down through the mountains to Lago di Garda; very scenic, *very* steep and very challenging in that ruddy Vauxhall!

When we arrived at the northern end of the lake, you were enchanted by the deep, clear waters and rugged rocky cliffs. It always gave me a glow when you were happy, that beaming smile on your face that I miss so much. After the calm of the mountains, the busy tourist areas of the lake were quite a contrast. We found a waterfront cafe and had a drink and a snack. I'd hoped to drive on the lakeside road for a while, but it was utter chaos. We decided that, to see the lakes properly, it would have to be early spring or autumn, so we headed back up into our peaceful mountains.

The next day, we ventured into the Italian Alps, close to the Swiss border. It was gorgeous, with quiet roads, stunning scenery and wonderful sights, especially the cows, with their enormous clanging neck bells. We stopped to look at the beasts, and got a tongue-licking from one we promptly named 'Doris' (don't ask!). We found a ski valley with the cable-car running to whizz hikers up to the summit for a scenic decent. We took our ski-cum-walking poles, and up we went. It surpassed the lake trip by miles! At the summit was a children's play area with life-sized carved wooden animals. A sign pointed towards a welcoming Alm cafe twenty minutes away – well, thirty for us. The Alms are charming mountain restaurants, usually built of logs and renown for hearty fare for skiers and hikers. We made it, and grabbed a table on the deck overlooking what in the winter would be the piste. We pictured skiers pushing off from here in great clouds of powdered snow. You were hoping for your favourite, goulash soup, but alas this was Italy, not Austria. I think we had some kind of pasta, but the scenery was the star of the trip. Oh, and Doris! Memories, my darling, that is all there is left now, and Doris is one of them; the multi-coloured china cow figure with a bell on a bow round her neck, that we chose from that cable-car station shop. Doris has been with us a long time now.

As our stay in Italy drew to a close, we would head back to Salzburg, hopefully change to a better car, and move on to our second timeshare resort. This was one of our favourites – The Alpen Club in Schladming. More on wonderful Austria later, but we did pop back to Avis at the airport and swap to a Mercedes B class. Ahh! Your hubby was a happy bunny again.

22

GRIEF, THE HARDEST THING

Now, I've been pondering how much I should say about some aspects of my grief for you, my darling. I have been told that others in our situation may find reading this helpful... So I have to tell them about The Demons. In the early days, the demons were prevalent, nearly hourly, triggered by a thought or memory or the simple wish that I could have done more to ease your suffering. When the demons come, especially in the depths of the night – the despair, the loneliness – there is only one weapon in my armoury: a happy thought, Peter Pan style. Thank goodness there are so many to chose from. Our numerous holidays, family gatherings, and just strolling hand in hand along the prom. The other aid to keeping me sane is the picture wall; the corner of the lounge where your hospital bed once lay is now adorned with many photographs, printed on canvas, of some of our best adventures. I gaze upon them for hours. You are always smiling! Boy, did we have some adventures. Not bad for a blind lady and a fat bloke.

I suppose this might be a good time to mention kids, or rather, the lack of them. We never really talked about having any. I think not meeting until we were both over thirty, we sort of naturally thought it was not an option. Plus, in those early years, I was hardly a great role model for fatherhood! You had yet to darn this old sock. We did touch on the subject in later years, usually over a wine or two in the summerhouse. You said I would have been a great father. I think you were wrong for once; we were too set in our selfish ways. But who else did we have to please? I remember us saying that any offspring we had would be a blind, arthritic, overweight cripple, and that was our way of not dwelling on it. But as a consolation we had (and still have), some wonderful nephews and nieces that you simply adored. You would sometimes tell me of the times you looked after them for the odd weekend, before I came along, and there was pure joy in your voice. God bless them.

This morning I sat down and wrote the Christmas cards. Not something I thought I would be doing again, but they're from St Barnabus, so all in a good cause. It was a job you used to love/hate, but there were so many more to write back then. I'm going up to Bruce and Cathy's for lunch on Christmas Day, as my brother has the space for all of us. That will be the extent of my Christmas – no decorations, or our favourite seasonal movies... I just can't do it.

23

FAMILY, BLESS 'EM

Tomorrow I'm going to Rutland to see the cousins. Kathy is coming, and we're giving her friend Janet a lift. I've rented a cottage near Rutland Water. I hope I can get along with Kathy for three days, we haven't been together for more than an hour or two in years, and I'm Mr Grumpy to her Mrs Fussy! This trip was one of the reasons for changing the car – yes, *again,* I hear you say, but when the girls talked of luggage, and seeing their disappointment at the T Roc's small boot, it set the wheels in motion for getting the Honda CRV. It's a lovely car, the auto being pure joy! Blimey, I have just realised that back in your heyday you could have driven it on your automatic-only licence!

Rutland was one of our last trips together in the spring of 2021, you'd lost your sight by then, but we could still get out and about. We stayed in a wooden lodge, in the grounds of a charitable institution. I took you to Barnsdale Gardens, the original home of Gardeners World. Luckily, it was wheelchair friendly. I described it all to you and held flowers for you to smell their delightful scents... That was a nice day. On the

Sunday, Dorian and Carole gave us a royal welcome, with Dorian donning his pinny and producing a superb roast beef lunch. Dave and Ann joined us and I believe there was even a choice of three desserts. After lunch we chatted in the conservatory, and you were in your element. No doubt there will be a few tears at those memories, this weekend. Winter has arrived now with a vengeance, and after an unusually mild autumn it was minus 4 last night. It's forecast to be one or two degrees over the weekend – not your sort of weather, my dear! But if there was still an 'us,' I expect we would have been off to Spain after Christmas. That holds no attraction for me now. Although, when Ventura was moored in Funchal, I did think I might like to revisit Madeira again. Sometime. Possibly.

I'm safely home now. The Honda was very comfortable for the journeys; six hours to do 180 miles, typical traffic for a Friday on the British motorways. The Rutland cottage was lovely, modern and well-heated, much to Kathy's relief. We had a pub meal with Carole and Dorian, a lovely turkey dinner, but we did have to wait an hour for it.

On Saturday we saw Dorian playing Father Christmas in his daughter's shop. The girls went to a garden centre in the afternoon, so Dorian and I had a real heart-to-heart. That was nice. Sunday saw Dorian in his pinny again, with a tasty roast the end result. Snow was forecast overnight, with dire warnings for travellers on Monday, but as it turned out we practically flew back in four hours. Hats off to Henry Honda.

Now, so far I haven't talked about your medical negligence case – mainly because it seemed to be dragging on forever. We were told that it would be a good idea to proceed, so nobody else would suffer from the same procedural errors that would come to haunt us. It's too painful to give all the details, but basically your 2016 scans were not acted on properly and if they had been, my dearest darling, you could have been cured. Oh boy, was that hard to hear and take in. Enough. On Friday afternoon in the cottage, our solicitor rang. The NHS Trust would not contest the case, and it would all be over soon with an interim payment in January! I started thinking about all the things I could do with those funds in your memory; St Barnabus, your beloved Women's Institute, the local food bank... And I would be secure, even if my health were to deteriorate further. Then I realised *why* there might be payments, and that brought me back down to earth in a flood of tears.

Then on Monday I heard that the NHS were insisting on probate! Which of course I don't have – why would I? There was just the two of us old socks, no kids and no complications. So of course I am now more depressed than ever, with up to six months more flapping around before I can dispose of all the horrible memories and all the files on your torturous illness. Damn them.

Now, I've no interest in saving for a rainy day. My health is terrible; an obese, depressed alcoholic is my diagnosis, darling. Perhaps there will be shed loads of money coming in, but without you it means nothing. Unless I can do some good with it, as well as please myself. The lovely couple I used to have an early evening drink with on the Canaries cruise booked to go on Arcadia in August, to Norway and Iceland. You know I always liked to have something on the calendar to look forward too. Iceland was always on our wish list, particularly that thermal blue lagoon... And so many other places were, too, my poor beloved. I'm tempted to book it. It might serve as an inducement to loose weight and get a bit fitter. Truth be told, I don't know what to do to ease my torment. There was only ever you. We were one.

Well, that's Christmas and New Year over, and I have finally got a seat in the Beach Bar. There's an awful lot of cold and flu bugs around as well as COVID-19 being on the rise. It's thought that the lock downs might be to blame, by denying people the natural herd immunity for two years. I've had a stinker of a cold and sinusitis over the whole festive (ha ha!) season – I never went anywhere or did anything. To round it all off, on New Year's Eve the probate forms arrived. Then a leak from the redundant chimney breast in the kitchen dripped out and destroyed the cupboard unit in the alcove... Happy New Sodding Year!

I was already unimpressed with the probate solicitor. She sent an email on Christmas Eve to say the registrar may have an issue with your will, my darling. Apparently you signed it twice. Angrily I replied, did they not realise you were totally blind by then, and even writing was a struggle? Your first attempt strayed out of the signing box, so you made a second successful attempt. Money or not, I am becoming heartily sick of the whole process, especially as the NHS Trust are not disputing the case. It now seems to be a barrage of petty box-ticking holding things up. I just want to concentrate on our wonderful life together, and not keep being dragged back into remembering that last horrible year.

Next week, on Monday the 9th of January, I am treating our lovely neighbours, Sandra and Dave, and Gail and Graham, to four nights at Warners Lakeside as a thank-you for being so supportive. I know you'd approve, darling. In typical Sod's Law fashion, Dave tested positive for COVID yesterday, with a week to go!

I am in the Beach Bar now, tapping away, and the lovely Kat and Sue are both telling me how illness over the holidays has spoiled their plans. Such a shame, they work so hard and deserve their downtime. To be honest, their welcome smiles and chats are one of the main reasons I come here most days.

After all that empty time over Christmas, and feeling really down, I've come to the realisation that, even with no major money worries, I am still as miserable as sin. If I was poor as well, life would be unbearable and pointless, or so it seems. So if the medical negligence case comes to nothing, I may well be joining you soon, my beloved. Death does not scare me, only the manner of it. A lingering decline in loneliness is my biggest fear. If the case is resolved though, the compensation can give me motivation to do some good with it. Your WI, St Barnabus, 4 Sight and the local food bank could all benefit, and that would give me a reason to carry on.

24

JUST WOBBLING ON

I did at one stage think of going to all our wish-list exotic locations; Canada, New Zealand... but I think I would be just as miserable. Still lonely, but a long way from home, as well. The cruises are great, and provide a good writing environment, but I keep coming back to the idea of a motorhome. Just like we used to have – big enough to go away for a few weeks, and be comfortable.

There is a lot that needs doing around the home as well. In fact, if there's no compensation life is going to get tough. The garden fences are rotten, the garage roof is leaking, the log borders are rotting away. There's a lot to do indoors too, ideally. I must start being a bit more frugal – he says, having booked two more cruises!

Linda, Christmas was terrible. The TV was dire beyond belief, and not being able to go out, I sat at the computer and looked at cruises. P&O of course, as our – I suppose now, *my* – loyalty level gives many discounts. I wrote a list of all the cruises I liked the look of until September 2023, and then proceeded to pretend to book them to get a price. The thought of an inside cabin after we always savoured the luxury of a balcony was too much to contemplate.

My research paid off; two cruises came out as not appearing to have the dreaded single supplement, a surcharge that compounds the misery of losing a loved one, damn them!

So, at our traditional holiday time of your birthday in June, I'll be on the smaller, adults-only Arcadia to the Baltic. I'll visit Norway, Sweden, Poland and Denmark, with Russia being off-limits at the moment. In February, I'll be taking the huge Ioana to Hamburg, scene of our first ever cruise (with Cunard). I hope I can cope with the larger ship, but it was ridiculously cheap – £780 for the week, with a balcony, free parking and £110 on board spends! Too good to miss. I suspect that by the time it comes around, I will really be ready for it.

Meantime, it will be housework, and trying to get the garden in shape. If it stops raining. The damn foxes have made a right mess of your memorial rose garden, but your special rose is untouched. I have now set all the 'boys' around it for protection – our long-lived garden ornaments, Percy Pig, Henry Hippo and the tortoise from your mum and dad's garden. Hopefully they can dissuade the foxes from your 'Simply the Best' rose. But no, that did not work, so I have bought more rose bushes to fill the gaps where all the frost bitten geraniums were. I've used my spare wood and some chicken wire to protect it all… It looks like Stalag 13 out there!

It's the weekend now, so housework today, then packing tomorrow ready for Warners on Monday. The weather is pretty terrible; high winds and rain, but it looks like it will be fine on Monday. At least we can move in without getting soaked. I hope I can be sociable for four days, it's been a long time since I've had an experience like this. With us it was so different, being so sympatico that we'd rarely have any differences of opinion about what to do or see. I do wonder though, at times, if you just went along with me to make life easy? It's horrible, the things you think about sometimes. It makes me wonder and question so many things, but of course there will never be answers, now. So I'd best stop driving myself mad.

Well! I'm back from Warners now, my dear. It was nice to have some company for a change, though sadly the weather was horrendous. Gales, and rain of Biblical proportions; no shooting, archery or boules for us. But Gail bought along a card game called 'Uno,' which everyone was able to play. I enjoyed it so much I ordered a pack from Amazon yesterday. You were greatly missed, my darling, and you would have loved the banter. It also made me aware of how hard it is for both Gail and Sandra, coping with their husbands, Graham and Dave. Breakfast at 9am was too early for them some days, and they didn't attend. I couldn't get to grips with writing in the room, comfortable as it was. I didn't think it would go down well sitting there writing, while the others played cards!

It was a break though, and a change of scenery. Warners said they were changing the menus – rubbish! The same tired, repeating menus, just now nearly everything is self-service – our pet hate, my darling! I never minded getting yours, but you always preferred us to be waited on. Of course, you being unable to see what is *in* the buffet added another dimension of hell for you. The girls really enjoyed not cooking though, and this was their first time for the menus. Monday, gammon; Tuesday, turkey. Wednesday, pork, Thursday beef. Which we all said was a lovely piece of meat. But I've been about ten times now, and nothing ever changes! You know it doesn't take much to irk me. I don't think I'll go back for a while. The cruise to Hamburg is up next; four weeks today, wow.

I go back to the craft club at St Barnabus on Monday, my first time in ages due to the holidays. I look forward to seeing the guys again. On Wednesday I'll restart the Arun Wellbeing course. The terrible weather and lack of exercise has seen me put on ten pounds, I'm now the heaviest I have ever been and my mobility is being affected. It looks like being cold but dry for a little while, so I've charged the bike's battery and am yearning to get out on it. Oh my darling, you would have been over the moon to be able to ride an e-bike! Back when you could see well enough to ride, we could have gone for miles, as we always lived close to the sea and the promenades. Oh, how I miss you. I'm really not sure how long I can carry on.

You would be proud of me darling, I went to Arun wellbeing, run by a nice girl called Natalie. She's lost seven stone already, so she knows what she's doing. It is a bit daunting, fifteen ladies and four of us blokes. I missed week one, so had to go barefoot on the super scales. 21 stone 8.2 pounds... Ouch! My metabolic age is 81. I'm surprised the scales didn't scream, "Get off you fat old git!" Natalie weighed everyone else, and then announced that everybody had lost something in the last week. So, a bit of incentive there then! I really must make this work.

Now for some good news: Eleri, our solicitor for your negligence case, called, on her last day before maternity leave. She'd spoken to the NHS Trust and they have agreed to an interim payment within four weeks! Oh darling, you are still looking after me, even now. Initial euphoria soon chilled when I remembered what the money is for... Probate will be another few months, and I still have no idea of what the final claim figure will be. Then there will be 'negotiations'... haggling over what your life was worth, my darling. Argh!

But in the meantime, I can breathe a sigh of relief financially. The flat and garden have deteriorated over the last couple of years. I want to get some things done in March, a doldrums month, before going to Cornwall around my birthday. I want to replace the condensation-filled kitchen and bedroom windows, renew the rotting border fence and fix the leaking garage roof. Then I can start getting the garden back into shape, so you'd be proud of it once more. In the long term, the kitchen needs a bit of work, and its floor, and the bathroom floor. Really, the whole place could use a spruce up, but it is comfortable enough for me so time will tell. All these little projects will give me a purpose, and hopefully get me fitter. It's still so damn cold, though! I tried a little walk, but it is only just above freezing and it took my breath away.

25

OFF WE GO AGAIN

Right girl! It's about time we went down memory lane again. I was watching 'Cruising with Susan Calman' on Sunday night, about a trip around Greece. I like her, but she's not a patch on Jane McDonald, who we both loved. Susan is too shouty and screechy, like Zoe Ball; it drives you mad, but the travels are great. She went around some of the inland villages in Greece and Crete, and there they were: the 'Black Hatters'. A term we coined in *Two Clots in a Camper,* it started on my three months working in Corfu and continued on our honeymoon there in 1990. The world was very different back then. On rare days, when I got a few hours off from the bar and pool complex and use of the boss's very battered car, I used to love driving into the hills to have a beer or rough local wine (grassi) in the old village tavernas. The tables would be filled with old men, all booted out of the house for the day by their womenfolk. They would nurse a coffee or retsina, playing dominoes and chatting, but mainly watching this bewildering new world of tourism encroach on their timeless old village. They were all shabbily dressed, in what was once their Sunday best, with scuffed shoes and always a black hat!

We saw the same characters on our honeymoon. We hired a Suzuki open-topped jeep, along with Angie and her boyfriend. She was an ex-holiday rep, and very, um... exuberant! Over several wines, and plates of those gorgeous Greek cheese pies – triangles of filo pastry filled with goats cheese – we decided to hire the jeep through the town mayor. He also owned the restaurant, and inevitably, he had this cousin…

The jeep turned out to be fairly new, and as I knew the roads we didn't expect any problems. We spent a few days touring some of the remote beauty spots, and had a fantastic time. But darling, like you, my biggest memory of the trip was Angie. Every time we hit a bump or pot hole she would shout, "Whoopaa!" at the top of her voice! What the old boys made of it, I dread to think. But from then on, every time we sat and watched the world go by, we would don our imaginary black hats and join those old boys…

That's virtually a full time occupation for me, now.

I don't know if you've been sending me physic messages (or nags!) from on high, but last week I had a dental check up and de-scale. All good, and surprisingly they hadn't knocked me off their lists after 18 months. Then today I went to Boots for an eye test. That was a bit hard, as it was a regular haunt of yours. But they were all lovely, especially Stephanie… Of course, they all talked about you. I have two new pairs of reading glasses on order, but everything else is unchanged, although I did struggle slightly with the field test on my left eye. The terminology is all too familiar after thirty years of eye hospital visits with you, my love. But at least they really did pull out all the stops for you. So I guess that's my 'MOT' done – well, apart from the get-fit-and-lose-weight bit. But I'm determined to try. You've seen to it that I have no money worries, now I must try to enjoy it, and hopefully, do a bit of good with it.

Now, Tony James Slater, my celebrated author friend in Australia, has been giving me advice on my writing, which I welcome. I hope he might use his skills to create a book cover for me, as he's a good mate. Tony says a book should have a theme, or a thread, that weaves its way through the script, reminding the reader of its purpose and keeping it in their focus. I've thought about this, and I believe my scribblings do indeed do that. The central point is two people so synchronised together that they virtually become one entity – then the journey when that relationship is ripped apart. The grief journey, the realisation of loss, trying to come to terms with the reality of daily life without you my darling, my soul mate, my other old sock. It really is shit. You told me, and all our friends, that you wanted me to 'have a life.' Well, Lindy Lou, that is so easy to say, but my god, so hard to do. Cruises, rental apartments, Warners… None of these make me happy, but they are a distraction, and a chance to write. I do enjoy driving, and this Honda CRV is super (apart from the 25 mpg around town!). So I think that a few road trips around the UK may be a good idea. I've discounted a campervan; things have really changed since COVID, both the vehicles and the pitches are super expensive, and I really don't think I'm physically up to camping anymore. But I will really miss having a toilet on board! Hmm… I wonder if I could have a porta-potti instead of one of the back seats? Just joking! Or am I…?

Well my dear, I am pleased to say that today, 27th January (just to put some point of reference in), it was finally nice enough to get outside. I put the heater on in your summerhouse to help chase the damp away, and then proceeded to fill up the garden waste bin before bin day on Tuesday. The three patches of pampas grass that normally survive the winter were all wilted and yellow; they alone filled the bin. None of the geraniums survived this year, so it is a good chance to rethink some of the garden. I am very pleased to tell you that the Simply the Best rose that Andy sent down has survived, despite the fox's best efforts to dig it all up. So I think I will turn that central raised bed into purely roses. I look forward to it warming up a bit to get really stuck in.

Two weeks tomorrow, I shall be off on P&O's Iona to Hamburg. I'm interested to see what I make of this ocean giant; they're certainly cheaper, due to the economies of scale, I suppose. One thing I must do on this trip is actually read what I have written so far and do a bit of editing, if needed. It would be naive to think it's all right the first time.

26

THE COPPARDS IN BOPPARD

Now my darling, where should our trip down memory lane take us next? Austria is the obvious choice, as we went so many times and loved the mountains. Not to mention Goulash soup, your favourite! I even got a recipe for it online and used to make it for you in the winter, complete with tiny, square, fried potato croutons. By golly it was good, based on an 8-hour slow-cooked pork shoulder, though it wasn't quite the same without the Alpine backdrop. Sadly, this dish is another one that I can't bring myself to make – like, I rarely have the pasta that you used to love so much... Silly, isn't it?

Following on from your Goulash, my dear, it leads nicely into one of our magical road trips – through the channel tunnel, overland to Boppard on the Rhine, following that mighty river down into Austria. Oh, how we loved it.

Our car at the time was ideally suited to a grand tour. Of course, all our vehicles had to have a name, and being Spanish we went with 'Pedro'. A Seat Altea Sport turbo diesel, a great fun motor for such a trip and economical to boot. We crested the hill above the ancient town of Boppard, with Roman remains laid out before us like something from a fairy tale. A vine-covered hill rose up from the Eastern town border, complete with a small, swaying, open-seat chairlift. Huge craft plied the wide ribbon of the Rhine, laden with everything from combine harvesters to containers, and floating hotels with gawping tourists lining the balconies and railings. I'd used Booking.com to get us a room at Hotel Garni Gunther, right on the riverfront. There was even a disabled parking bay right outside! You were absolutely enthralled with the place. We checked in and were pleased to be on the top floor, with a large picture window overlooking the river. Our accommodation was what they call a 'Hotel Garni,' meaning it only served breakfast. This suited us down to the ground. It was early afternoon and we hadn't eaten, so we wanted to seek out a local-style place to eat tonight. I think we were booked in for three nights, and for two more on our return leg. It's details like this that your amazing memory would have recalled in an instant; I think it was probably April, around my birthday.

A few yards from our hotel on the river front, a few people were gathered around a stall from which delicious aromas were emanating. A 'Sausage Shack.' which was common and very popular in Germany and Austria. There was only one item to choose from: *Bratwurst mit Brot,* with both mild mustard and ketchup. Absolutely scrumptious! The thick, meaty sausage in a white finger roll was an experience we would repeat many times on our travels, and it was cheap to boot!

We sat on a bench enjoying our bratwurst, as the constant flow of river traffic passed us by. This was ideal 'black hatting' territory. Two-hundred yards downstream was a small foot passenger ferry that would take us over to the far bank, where the railway from Cologne whizzed by at regular intervals. We had no idea that, one fine winter's day, we too would be passengers on a Great Railway holiday to Switzerland. From this side we got some great photos of the town and our picturesque hotel, and found a sign with the town's name, Boppard. I got you to stand under it and hey presto, we had our 'Coppards in Boppard' moment captured.

Back on the East Bank we wandered the beautiful old town area, and found a nice *Wien Staub* that looked like a good bet for dinner. Strolling back towards the hotel we came across a *Tee Haus*. It looked like something from a film set, gaily painted with leaning walls and a crooked roof. We went in and enjoyed a pot of tea and fairy cakes on small, delicate chinaware. Lovely! But now I was definitely overdue a German beer!

That evening we went to the Restaurant, *Severus Stube,* that we'd found that afternoon. It was smokey inside but mixed with a wonderful aroma of cooking meat drifting from the kitchen. We were surprised to be seated on a long table with other people, as was the norm in these places. We made small talk as much as possible, with a bit of sign language thrown in. Of course, the menu was just a chalkboard on the wall, in German. Using our guide book we ordered the dish of the day, a hearty bowl of beef stew – and of course, boiled potatoes. Always boiled potatoes! Two large steins of beer appeared, a delicious local golden ale. Dessert was simple, as apple strudel was easy to spot. It was light and buttery, a far cry from the frozen ones we get at home. It was a lovely evening. Back at the hotel, the owner spoke good English and we discovered we could buy a cold bottle of local Rhine wine and take it up to the room. This was a pattern we'd repeat throughout our stay. We pulled up chairs and sipped the wine looking out at the never-ending river traffic, feeling pretty contented with ourselves.

The next day, after a breakfast of fresh bread, boiled eggs and coffee, we drove along the riverbank to see some of the other towns. Around lunchtime we found a sausage shack in the middle of nowhere. After using sign language and a few nods, we were handed paper plates with two bits of cheap sliced bread, a dollop of mustard and ketchup, and two hot dog sausages. A paper cup of coffee each came out as well. You went to the bench with the plates, while I held out a ten-euro note and a handful of coins. I was amazed when he took just three euros, so I left another one on the counter. We expected not to enjoy this basic fare, but actually we loved it!

The following day, we took a boat ride to see the famous Loreley Statue and the many breath-taking castles overlooking the enormous waterway. it was a very scenic experience. The imposing Pfalzgrafenstein Castle sits in the middle of a narrow stretch of river, a huge wedge of stone seemingly driving through the water. The Robber River Barons, as they were called, used to run huge chains over to both banks, forcing unlucky travellers and traders to pay a toll. On our return, we took a car ferry to the far bank and drove to the island where the Loreley Statue sat. We walked down the rough path to get close up photos of it, then drove up to a high viewpoint to get some amazing panoramic pictures.

At the northern edge of Boppard, a vineyard sits on a bend in the river. An open-topped, two-seat cable car whisked us up to the cafe and viewpoint above the vines. I'm not normally bothered by heights, but this one really got to me. I hated it – but you, Bonkie The Intrepid, never batted an eyelid. I did wonder if not being able to see too well was an advantage on that swaying, rickety old Sesselbahn!

27

BAD GASTEIN

Next morning we tackled the long drive to Austria. The first part is spectacular, running beside the Rhine with castles nearly every mile. Then Industrial Germany hits, after which you're over the border and back in the mountains. Passing beautiful Lake Zell, we drove on the quiet eastern side, avoiding busy Zell am See. Soon we entered the gorgeous Gastein Valley. Our timeshare was at the far end, high in the mountains, in the spa town of Bad Gastein. The Hotel Mondi clings to the mountainside, overlooking the town and the snow-capped peaks far to the west. As part of a spa complex, the apartment is of the highest quality, with large windows looking out on the view. Do you remember, we loved those Austrian beds – huge feather duvets you could snuggle down into, whilst gazing at the stars over the mountains. Wunderbar!

The complex had the most wonderful spa facilities. We had many lovely dips in the swimming pool-sized Jacuzzi; it was kept at 30 degrees, even hot enough for you, my dear. I would leave you soaking in the warmth and venture into the main, much cooler swimming pool for a few lengths, before dashing back to join you. We were self catering, which we liked as it was more economical, allowing us to save our money and treat ourselves to the occasional meal out.

Past the town, a high mountain road leads up to a rather unusual railway terminal. Cars get loaded onto the train, and a long tunnel takes them right through the Eastern Alps to Italy! We never did it, but it did sound exciting. After the station, even higher into the peaks, a wonderful valley unfolds – Sport Gastein, which even in April was a snowy wonderland. This was the high alpine skiing area, with a cable car and a weather station which we trudged up to through the snow. It was a lovely experience – Bonkie the Intrepid was back!

Back at the car park, two ladies were being pestered by a middle aged man. He was trying to get them to go in his car back to town; they were trying to say no, as they'd walked up using their ski poles. It was quite a trek, though. As you were with me, I thought they might prefer to come back with us, which in the end, they did. You kept glaring daggers at me and whispering, "How do you know where they want to go?" So I told you, "Um, they were in the giant Jacuzzi with us yesterday!"

Seeing as everyone except us was using ski poles to aid walking and prevent falls in this steep and icy town, we visited a ski shop and bought a pair each. On the way back, it must have been so obvious that we did not know how to use them! A kindly couple explained the technique as best they could. We had them much too short, like walking sticks, when they should be nearly chest-height. Then it goes, right foot, left stick forward, left foot, right stick forward. Going uphill, you push from a slight rearward position, and downhill have them slightly forward to stop a fall. I had a roll of white insulation tape in the 'breakdown box' in Pedro, which I wound around your canes, hoping people would realise they were also blind canes. The poles made such a difference that I still use them now, for Nordic walking on the prom at home.

Laying in bed last night in the early hours, I was trying to recall our many trips to the Alps; Austria, Switzerland and of course, oft-overlooked Bavaria – so many over the years. If I try to cover them all in one part of this book it might make readers loose interest, so I'll keep popping back and splice those tales with other titbits from our life and travels. Not having children, and both of us being employed full-time at EDF Energy – not to mention the savings we built up from various sources, including your wonderful parents – meant we could enjoy numerous holidays. We took every opportunity to travel, as there was always the possibility that your little bit of remaining sight would vanish one day. I take great comfort, darling, in the fact that in nearly every photo we have of you, you are grinning like a Cheshire cat!

So, back to Bad Gastein. Below our complex, the town stuck fast to the mountainside. A crashing river flowed under a stone bridge, fed by a towering waterfall that cascaded into a pool below the bridge. It sent up great clouds of spray – except on one of our visits, when it was actually frozen solid! We walked the tortuous trail up to the lip one time; the view from up there was glorious. I was always so proud of how you always attempted these things. With your limited vision it must have been scary... Or perhaps you couldn't see how perilous it was! We went there three times in all – cue your near-photographic memory – but my wine-addled brain can't recall exact dates, or even what we did on each trip. Nevertheless, all these memories are mixed up in there somewhere.

From the resort entrance it would have been quite a hike to the bridge area, which doubled as the town square, but by following others who were obviously going for a walk, we discovered a great short cut. If you took the lift down several floors to the ski lockers and changing rooms, there was a door to the town that cut the journey in half.

Bad Gastein is a renowned wellness resort, where people come to spend the day reclining in the old, slightly radioactive salt mine to improve their breathing and general health. Surprisingly, when most of them come back out into daylight, the first thing they do is light up a fag!

On the road in the upper part of town, by the train station, is another, less salubrious wellness hotel. Beside it, a cable car whisks skiers up to the high pastures in winter months. And opposite this is our all-time favourite swimming complex, complete with a wonderful cafeteria that serves ever-flowing Goulash soup!

There is an Olympic-sized pool for lengths and a smaller one that families tend to use. Plus the sauna and Jacuzzi of course, but it's the outside that is truly amazing; a lazy river feature that runs for about fifty yards each way, full of little bays with pulsing massage jets and tiled ledges to perch on. All at a balmy 28 degrees! Every twenty minutes or so, they speed up the flow for five minutes. It's amazing, you'd pay a fortune for this at a theme park back home. We loved it, didn't we darling. Another aspect you loved was the spacious disabled changing room that we could use together. Many places don't have a space suitable for couples like us who need to be together. After this invigorating experience we would retreat to the cafeteria… In fact, we'd often return here to eat in the evenings. It was very good food and excellent value. And if the weather was kind, the outdoor terrace provided stunning mountainside views.

Writing all this is making me realise how much I miss Austria and the Alps, but would it be enjoyable without you, my dear? Perhaps if I tried new pastures... But it's a long way to go to suffer a meltdown. That's one reason I book cruises, as I can't turn tail and run for home. Pathetic, I know.

From where we stayed in the beautiful Gastein Valley it's a short drive to another of our all-time favourite places, the Liechtensteinklamm gorge and falls near the charming Alpine town of St Johann im Pongau. This is a place where one of your many nicknames is well-earned, Bonkie the Intrepid! An unassuming woodland car park with a path to a ticket booth starts the exciting trek. An alm cafe with outside seating gave us a break for a coffee before our ascent – yes, ascent! We noted the Goulash soup on the menu for a hearty lunch afterwards.

Refreshed for our climb, we found the wooden trail that winds up the rocky gorge. It was barely twenty-feet wide, with the thundering torrent of water right beside us. Fallen pine trees caused log jams and created mini waterfalls; if there's been recent rain, the rushing waters can be truly terrifying. White stick in hand, you felt your way up the slippery wooden trail, stopping where possible so you could scan in the view while I took photos. I was so proud of you at times like this. We reached the end of the boardwalk to find a deep rocky pool set in a sun-drenched glade. The high cliff in front of us sent thousands of tons of water cascading down to fuel the stunning Klamm gorge. The trek back down was a little harder for you; I guided you as always, and holding hands was second nature for us. The Goulash soup was your reward for a beautiful but challenging morning out, bless you.

28

HAMBURG CRUISE

I'm cruising again, my dearest! Iona this time, with 5,200 passengers! It's school half-term holidays, I cocked-up there. We're visiting Hamburg; I'm there now, sitting in a bar, typing away. The weather is grey and gloomy, and our monstrous ship is berthed out of town in the docks, ugh. Our beloved Ventura is in sight, in a dry dock for her yearly spruce up. I wish we'd moored where we did when we were on the Queen Elizabeth, right next to the city. I won't waste much time writing about this trip, I hate it... all families and sideshows, it reminds me of being in a theme park. It's day three and I haven't spoken to a soul. I've got to think long and hard about June's Baltic cruise. But at least that one's on little Arcadia, and adults-only, thank goodness. By contrast, this is a mega ship and very modern. Remember, we were on Ventura in the Mediterranean when they announced the name, and a big party night followed. The ship being modern is nice, but there is no charm. If you stuck to the central walkways, you wouldn't even know you were sailing.

My balcony cabin at first glance seems superb and the much larger bathroom with a proper shower cubicle is lovely. But actually the cabin is quite cramped, and I'm constantly stubbing toes and banging hips. You would have been black and blue, my love! Stupidly, they've done away with drawers, so all the socks and undies just roll around on shelves. There's very few older folk, so I keep myself to myself. I'm now thinking that exploring Britain in a camper van might be the way to go. There's been a series on TV recently, Weekend Escapes with Robson Green, all around Northumberland and Cumbria. It looks so beautiful and peaceful. Not a new housing estate on every bit of space like at home, damn them! Ruining our lovely town, they are, gridlock everywhere. Took me two and a half hours to do the fifty miles to Southampton on Saturday, Lord knows the hell we'll face in the summer.

I am probably made more miserable by the fact that I can't drink. The last two years have finally caught up with me. More than one drink a day and my kidneys scream 'Stop,' making me shuffle around like an old man in pain... Which I am. This doesn't paint a very good picture of me, does it Lin? I am way overweight, and my horrible umbilical hernia sticks out further every week. I have to change, or die. A bit of a toss-up at the moment, but if I give up the wine, I might have a chance. I know you wanted me to have a life, but I am not sugar-coating anything in this book. That wouldn't be right; I'd say the truth to you if we were talking in our wonderful summerhouse. This is also a story of my grieving process. Until I joined the bereavement classes at St Barnabus, I thought many of the things I have experienced were unique to me. Not so! And retelling the journey truthfully might just help someone else in the same horrid situation. I felt so sad before I sat down here to write. I'm in The Glass House, by the way, the upmarket Olly Smith wine bar. The tables are at writing height!

I did a lap of the promenade deck. I try to walk a lot every day, so I get to see a lot of the ship. There are little three-person Jacuzzis dotted around the place, dozens of them, and some wonderful infinity pools at the stern. How I long to be able to use one. Many are empty today, with people in town, but I'm so conscious of my disgusting body shape that I didn't even pack shorts this time. I did take them on the last two cruises, but never had the courage or privacy to have a dip. I keep using my grief and your tragic demise as an excuse for my state, but that is just plain wrong. Maybe after a few days with little or no alcohol, my mind is starting to clear and focus again.

Before I came on this cruise, I visited our local food bank, The Pantry, in the church hall. Patricia, one of our older lady neighbours that I shop for, had been urging me to offer my help for weeks. I went to Lidl for jars of coffee, tea bags, basmati rice and some multi-bags of little sweets for any kids, and I took my offerings around last Wednesday. I was impressed by our local folks and the way they ran the bank. People could choose up to ten items, and I was pleased to see the clients didn't try to abuse the system. Once a month The Pantry opens early in the morning, and they lay on tea, coffee and croissants for the visitors. The lady vicar was flitting from table to table… it was all so nice, or as we would have said in our own personal made up language, 'chumbley'. I will do what I can for them in future, which is quite a bit thanks to you my darling, though it also saddens me. I don't think anyone on board here is suffering the current financial squeeze that so many are feeling at home, although I suspect many of them on board are the very public servants bringing chaos to the country by their strikes. Probably a few train drivers too! Right, stop there Grumpy, don't get started!

It looks like your medical negligence case might be drawing to a close. They've coughed up a £30k 'interim' payment; I was elated, until I realised what it was for. Through their negligence, they let you die. That is very hard to write. They are still arguing over the final amount, and probate is still dragging on. I long to destroy all your medical files and emails, reminders of your tragic last year. That wasn't you, my upbeat, wonderful Linda. I long to recapture just our happy memories and our life together, but until it's finally over, I have to keep it all.

While on the subject of helping others, one major regret I have is not being quicker to take up the offer of 'night sitters,' to care for you in those impossible last weeks of illness. I'd worked myself to the point of exhaustion trying to care for you by myself, which was a mistake. It left me too tired to do what I really should have done; talk to you, and comfort you as much as possible. Of course, now I have countless things I want to talk about with you, but all too late.

Tomorrow is a sea day. There's an interesting lecture on space at 11am, but not much else of interest to me. I'm even getting bored with the casino! At least I'm still playing with P&Os money, they gave me a £250 voucher on the last cruise. Apparently I'm a 'Player'... that's probably not a good thing! Even the slot machines on this tub are boring, no roulette or any machines that require player input or skill, not even hold buttons. Just spinning reels of childish garish graphics, the only job the player has is to feed it money and press go! America has a lot to answer for, but it has saved me a few Bob. Albeit at the expense of one of my few pleasures.

Wednesday we stop in Rotterdam, then Zeebrugge and thankfully home. I must say, the lectures from the astronomy professor were extremely good – they're about the only event I've been to. There were lots of late comers and early leavers, which I consider damn rude, but that's the standard of many guests around here now. I must think hard about cancelling the June Baltic trip when I get back. P&O clearly don't want their old customer base anymore, a bit like the BBC and Radio 2. The trendy TV adverts should have warmed me of their new target customer base... Well, they're welcome to them. The last two cruises have not been enjoyable. I know most of it is down to me; I don't like the shows without you, I haven't even gone to bingo on here due to the crowds. It seems like writing this is the only thing that gives me any pleasure. But on this ship I can't find a quiet corner to compose in. The Metropolis bar during the day on Ventura was ideal, but everywhere here is rammed with people. I sit here now on the last day, with screaming brats running around, in the Glass House Bistro for Christ's sake!

This nightmare of a cruise isn't done with me yet. In an effort to change my drinking habits and cut back a bit, I decided to try a pint of lager before lunch and another after, to space it out a bit. A pink gin and tonic in the evenings (or two, max). All was fine until Friday afternoon. I'd packed and put my main suitcase out in the passage by 2pm as instructed. Noting that mine was the only one out there on time, I limped back into the cabin. What's going on? My left foot was starting to swell and become tender... Oh no, not gout again, not here! I laid on the bed with my foot on a cushion, hoping it would go away. Lin, I can just hear you saying, "Self-inflicted, I told you to stop drinking!" It got steadily worse, but I couldn't lay down all evening. I was determined to try to get on the roulette table for one last go, having hardly played at all this trip. I hobbled down to deck seven, then along to the casino at the bow end of this iron monster. Again, only one table was open and all the seats were taken. I do a spread of bets the whole length of the table, so I need to be seated. You would have thought it would be worth their while to open the second table, as I could see others wanting to play, but no. So I hobbled up to the Crows Nest, the piano and cocktail bar, for a G&T. There were a few kids in residence, but not the screamers from yesterday. After two drinks I went back to the casino, to the same scenario – no room at the inn. My foot was really painful by then, so I decided not to bother with dinner. I could hobble no more! Back at base I changed and, just leaving an overnight bag for the morning, I put my second little suitcase out for collection. In bed a few hours later, the pain was terrible. I couldn't even stand the weight of the quilt on my foot, and I was shivering with cold. I put on my anorak and opened the door to grab my suitcase for a Tee shirt, but it was gone. Back in bed with my coat on, I had a restless doze. I was missing you, darling, and feeling very sorry for myself. Then came the sweats... Sorry, I did say this tale would be warts and all! I was dripping, so was the pillow and quilt, and the pain was horrendous. I kept thinking, how the hell am I going to disembark? I'll need to get to the disabled persons meeting point and beg a wheelchair. Unfortunately, that's at the opposite end of the ship! I managed a shower, and abandoned all thoughts of going up for breakfast. I left the cabin at around 7.40am, before the 8 am deadline. Leaving early meant the lifts were quiet, so I headed down to deck 6 to begin the long trek. Midway there, I came across the gangway to get off. I asked the officer if the cases were ready to collect in the hanger on shore, and he said yes. I told him that I was en route to the disability meeting point, but it was probably the same distance if I got off and went to the hanger... He said, "Yes, much the same, and there is no queue yet." So I got off, hobbling like an old cripple down those endless ramps. I grabbed a trolley, which made walking much easier, got my cases and picked up my beautiful, comfy, AUTOMATIC Henry Honda. If Henry had been a manual gearbox, I could not have driven. Home at last, Volterol and Ibuprofen provided blessed relief. That afternoon I researched gout, and discovered that the two worst drinks for it are beer and spirits! Argh. If I'd stuck to my usual cider and wine, in moderation, I might have been ok!

P&O's Iona didn't suit me. It was like staying in Butlins for a week! I am definitely in the traditional cruising camp. However, I can see the attraction for families; great facilities, loads of pools and hot tubs, the shows and entertainments… For me, there were far too many children whose parents who didn't give a damn about keeping them in check. Such is today's world! Thank goodness this grumpy old git is coming to the end.

I really must get my head straight, and decide what I want to do before I waste more time and money. At least March will keep me busy, fitting new rear windows, a new fence, and getting your beautiful garden up to scratch. I am so lucky in so many ways… but also a little lost.

Now, my dear, where shall we venture to next in our recollections of holidays past? Blimey, that sounds like a line from Charles Dickens, A Christmas Carol! But then, I guess this is what I'm writing – the ghosts of adventures past. And I say again, we had a fair few.

29

PORTUGAL

Our trip to Portugal is a perfect example. We picked the charming riverside town of Tavira, not far from the Spanish border, as our destination. We flew into Faro with British Airways and picked up our Avis hire car, a Fiat Tipo. I was quite pleased as it made a change – that is until I discovered it was only 1000cc. As expected, it was not exactly nippy, but comfortable enough. Looking online (this was a few years ago), I'd found the Vila Gale via Expedia; a 4-star hotel in the centre of town, close to the river and its central Roman bridge. We had a great balcony with views over the river and estuary. The area around the bridge featured stalls and a bar, often hosting were art exhibitions or craft fairs. I recall an ornate pond, filled with terrapins basking in the sun. It really was a charming spot and the focal point of the town. We'd go out exploring and come back here to sit 'black hatting,' with a bottle of Vino Verde, the very new crisp, slightly bubbly white wine of the region. The west side of the square was lined with restaurants, their menus full of fresh fish, which you loved. The traditional colourful fishing boats were moored by the bridge and we watched boxes of today's catch being delivered straight to the kitchens. You can't get fresher than that! Some species were rather hideous looking, like the 'Espada' or scabbard fish, but you ate it just the same, while I stuck to swordfish or a stringy steak.

There's a large sandbar island just off the estuary, housing a derelict cannery from the days of huge sardine shoals. With those days a distant memory, the island is now a tourist attraction with great beaches. We took a ferry over one day, just as foot passengers. We discovered a second Vila Gale hotel set in the dunes, with a wonderful spa; the prices were the same as our room! Damn, got it wrong again. Huge anchors from ships scrapped long ago dotted the dunes like a forest, helping to hold the sand and grasses in place against erosion. There was even a small fun fair. It was quite a charming place. I can't recall if we had a swim or not... Again, your memory is required here, my dear.

In the mornings, we would have a drive and explore the area. We found a cliff-top village with a fort giving commanding views of the coast; I recall a windmill as well, with cloth sails like a ship. To the west of Tavira there was more of a holiday resort feel, with hotels overlooking the sandy beach, and the dunes with their fields of iron anchors. There was even a miniature railway that ran among the dunes... Did we go on it? I don't know. It was so long ago.

I do remember that bitch of a Dutch cafe owner! Oh, we were so angry and so bloody helpless. We'd stopped for lunch at her dune-side café. We fancied prawns and asked her if she had any. She said she would make us a special, so we thanked her and added two beers to the order. The beers were cold and refreshing, but then a tin party platter arrived. A plain green salad filled one end, bread the other, and in the middle was a pile of small shell-on prawns, swimming in dirty fryer oil. Why the hell would you deep-fry them? It was revolting. We picked at it, not wanting to hurt her feelings. Two young, well-dressed men sat at the next table looking at our meal with obvious disgust... I couldn't blame them. We asked for the bill and she bought it over. Seventy euros for the platter! What? We said that was far too expensive, but she just replied, "You pay, or I call police!" Knowing we could never fight our corner with the local police in English, we paid and left. Back at the car, the two young men approached us. They said, "That is not a good picture of our town, your meal was terrible, it was a trick! Follow us to see the tourist police and we will explain everything to them." So we did. The officers were very nice, and with their story told, we thanked the men and let them get back to work. We followed the police car back to the café, where we were told to stay in the car. The cops went to see the Dutch lady, but she shouted, waved her arms and pointed at us. We could practically feel the venom coming off the witch. The officers came back, apologised, and told us that this wasn't the first time they'd visited that café. The woman had said that we'd ordered a 'special,' not on the menu, so she could charge what she liked. They were powerless. So the lesson is, never go 'off piste' in a restaurant! Always ensure the price is visible. That kind of put a cloud over the trip, so I think I'll leave Tavira there. Such a shame, as it's a lovely town.

30

WOBBLE AGAIN

It was 1st of March yesterday. Laying in bed, trying to decide between Radio 2 and Greatest Hits Radio, it dawned on me that we can no longer enjoy another tradition. 'Pinch Punch' for the first of the month; if I got you first, you would reply with, 'a poke in the eye for being so sly'. I'm certain that we sometimes let each other win just to keep it even!

Today, 2nd March, is a big day. The fencers came this morning, and had twenty fence panels slotted in by 9.30am Very impressive. The panels are good quality, with proper joints on the corners rather than just nailed together. They're from Romania; it seems we can't even make fence panels in this country anymore! Now, my dearest Bongle, I can start getting the garden into shape. It was a very harsh winter, some of the plants that normally survive didn't make it. All the pampas grasses look like history, but I'm hoping they may pop back. I bought three healthy-looking Camellias in Lidl to fill some of the many gaps. You adored our beautiful garden, so I have to get it up to scratch in your honour.

Also, visitors love it, not that there are many of those now. I hope it warms up a bit soon, it is still really quite bitter outside; an hour or so is more than enough for me at the moment.

Lin, I must tell you this, talk about a small world. I had a zoom chat with our solicitor, Marianne, about your negligence case. They are now at the 'arguing the toss' stage over the figures. It seems you are still looking after me even now, it could be a month, or six, so I try not to think about it. I could see from the background that Marianne was at home, not the office, so I asked where she was. "Rutland," she replied. "Not near Oakham?" I asked. "Actually, I am in Oakham," she said. I told her that I have cousins there and visited a few weeks ago. At the end of the meeting I said, "I don't suppose the name 'Penfold' means anything to you?" "Do you mean Dorian and Carole?" she asked. "Yes!" I was somewhat flabbergasted. Their daughter, Jennifer, is one of my best friends! Spooky or what? But I also take that as a good omen for a successful and swift conclusion. Until the case is over, I still get dragged back to thinking of your terrible illness, instead of concentrating on our wonderful life together. I still have all the hospital paperwork and emails, and I long to put all that behind me.

I keep having thoughts, daydreams of getting a campervan again, but am I up to it anymore? I want to do some road trips in the UK and love the idea of having a base – not to mention a toilet while on the move! But would I just be a lonely old fart come the evenings? It would be great for writing, and taking my camera to capture the travels... hell, even the binoculars that Chris and Olwyn gave me for my birthday might finally get some use. But it is a lot of money to lose if I make yet another error of judgement. Perhaps when I know the final figure of settlement that will help me decide. I really need your voice of reason on topics like this Bongle, you always were the one to curtail my impetuous streak.

While I am in this self-pitying frame of mind, I shall mention food, or fuel as it is now. I used to love cooking for you; your favourites like Goulash soup, the many pasta dishes, stir fries and of course your favourite fish dishes. Now though, I find it hard to think of anything that I fancy. I remember you telling me before we met that beans on toast was your regular meal. It's fast becoming a staple of my diet, too! I keep buying salad stuff, with good intentions, but it is so damn cold still that it mostly gets binned. I might try a chicken salad today, although I suspect the addition of baked potatoes and beans will win out.

On Sunday all the Coppard clan are gathering for lunch up at Wickwoods Country Club. I set it up as we never got together at Christmas. I'm paying – or rather, you are, from the interim payment I received last month. I do hope it goes well, but with my lot you can never tell. I will keep you posted. Already Olwyn says Chris will probably not be well enough after his recent vocal chord operation, and young Henry is due to work. Ho hum, the best laid plans of mice and men etc.

31

SCHLADMING, AUSTRIA

Laying awake last night (not an unusual occurrence these days), I was pondering which destination to write about next. For some reason, 'Babies' Willies' leapt into my mind... 'What?' I can imagine the readers gasping, but we know, don't we darling! Although it did take us by surprise, the first time we had it; homemade pea and ham soup with tiny frankfurters in. You exclaimed, "Babies' willies!" Luckily, our hosts in the Alm did not speak a word of English!

The Alpine Club Hotel, set in the Eastern outskirts of Schladming, was a timeshare we returned to many times. Nestled on the hillside above a cable car station, the swaying cars ran right across the front of the hotel. Our apartment was always a superior one on the front of the building. Floor to ceiling windows across the lounge and bedrooms gave superb views of the valley, the cable car and on to the Dachstein Glacier. We loved it, but we had to make sure we drew the curtains if getting up while the cable car was running! We had a small kitchen, so breakfast was in the apartment and we would grab a bite (and a pint or two) while out for the day. In the evening, we'd go to the on-site restaurant or eat in. We loved roaming the supermarket shelves, finding all manner of meaty treats. Goulash being one of your favourites, along with a Semmel Knodel, or dumpling, to soak up the rich gravy. There was a wonderful indoor pool with saunas and a strange Jacuzzi bath that you had to put a coin in! The pool was warm enough for you, my dear, with nice easy steps; you hated when it was just a ladder. We must have looked a bit odd when swimming. It had to be very quiet; a crowded pool was a nightmare, and scary for you. If we had the pool to ourselves you could do your own thing. If there were others, we would do lengths, you following behind me with (as you said) my bald spot as a beacon to avoid you crashing into others! Oh baby, all these near forgotten things are being bought back to life by writing this. I do wonder what I will do once this gets completed. Mind you Bonkie, I have not even started on our camping adventures. My god, how did we find time to work!

32

TAKE FIVE

On Sunday, my dear, we treated the Coppard clan to Sunday lunch at Wickwoods Country Club, a venue we enjoyed many times as it was mother's favourite. Not having got together over Christmas, I thought it would be nice to see everyone, so I booked a table for eleven people for 1.30 pm. As the interim payment had come through on your negligence case, I thought I would say lunch is on you. When I booked it, I gave everyone a month's notice. Of course, anything involving the Coppards would not go to plan. Firstly, my brother Bruce's mother-in-law was busy, my other brother Chris has complications from a recent operation, so three down. Then my sister Kathy's cat was diagnosed as diabetic, just like our little Simba and so I thought her, James and Katie might be cancelling. Then it turned out that Bruce's son, Henry was working until 2pm, so I moved the booking to 2.30. Fearing I might be sitting alone at a table for eight, I thought much wine might be required, so I booked a room upstairs for the night. I know, I can hear you telling me off from on high! But if you were still here, my dear Bongle, I would not need the wine. Well, not so much anyway.

I arrived at 1.30pm and went up to the room to drop off my case. It was very spacious, with a small separate area with a desk and wardrobe; nice for writing, I thought. And a good bathroom; not bad for £110. I'm not going away in March, so that was my justification. But my fears were unfounded. The eight of us had a table at the far end of the restaurant; service was a bit below what it used to be, but acceptable nonetheless. The meal was very nice, we all had roasts and desserts, and the two boys opted for burgers. I saw them off around 4.30pm and had a final glass of wine by the roaring fire in the bar area. I had relaxing evening reading the paper, then watched a couple of things on TV and had a nice time. Breakfast was superb. I opted for two poached eggs on toast and crispy bacon. The eggs were cooked to perfection, a rarity. On the surprisingly trouble-free drive home I popped into Rustington Windows and paid the deposit for the bedroom and kitchen window replacements. They don't even make them anymore; they buy them in, made to measure, from Eastern Europe! This country does nothing itself anymore. It always niggled us when we bought the flat that they had renewed the front and side windows, but not the back. Oh well, now they'll be done. As I get older and more decrepit – self-inflicted, I know dear – I feel the need to future-proof the place as much as possible. Now the fence is done, the windows ordered, and a new shower enclosure arrives this week. Little by little, it gets done, and it keeps me busy. I hate having time to dwell on what might have been. More came from the solicitor today: final papers to sign, and a horrible account of our future hopes and plans had that bloody cancer not got you. Well, to be truthful it's got us both. I try to stop drinking, loose weight and get fit, but then I just think, why? Perhaps I'll try again when the weather picks up. Duck! Flying pig alert!

Back to Schladming. There was so much to do in this area; numerous walking trails were literally just up the road behind the hotel. One especially springs to mind, for good and bad reasons. When we drove up that winding road in high summer, the farmer charged a toll, as many do. There was a car park and a circular walk on the hillsides above a small lake, but best of all, at the halfway point was a cute little alm. The wife was an amazing baker, the strudel, cakes and pastries were scrummy. Grabbing our ski poles we set off around the western side of the lake. Young goats along with chickens could be seen in pens by the water near the alm, their eggs no doubt going into the baker's bowl. We reached the alm with no other customers around, so we took the outside bench with a view over the water. We ordered hot chocolate, our regular drink when hiking, and two wedges of a rich chocolate cake. The host even took our photo for us; it's on canvas on the lounge wall at home. That's my sanity wall, darling – pictures from many of our adventures, that I had made into canvas prints as a constant reminder of our wonderful travelling life together.

Refreshed, we could linger no longer. We had two choices: return to the car park, back along the track to the road and the car, or the more adventurous trail, skirting the farm opposite along the hillside and dropping back through the farmyard to the carpark. We decided on the scenic route; Bonkie the Intrepid was back again, bless you. The climb above the farm was higher and tougher than we'd thought, and definitely a lot longer! Eventually we reached the farm, with just the yard to cross to get back to the car. Unfortunately the cows had just crossed the yard for milking, so it was a quagmire – as I am sure you recall, darling. "It'll be slippy," I warned you, "but with your two sticks acting as second legs, you can't fall over." Famous last words... Halfway across, your ski pole slid out from under you and down you went, face first! Oh my dearest Bonkie, you were covered, and in what we dare not think! You even managed to loose one of the rubber tips from a pole, as well. Eventually we did laugh about it, but not for a few days. You, your clothes and the car took a lot of cleaning! From there on in, we avoided farms like the plague. Oh my dear, we did have some fantastic adventures! I suspect that's why it's so hard to find something that gives me pleasure. Cruises, trips... I just don't know. I am starting to realise that a camper van would also be an expensive disappointment.

A few miles to the east of Schladming there's a road that winds up through the green fertile slopes, with cows grazing all around, their bells clanging as they bend to devour the lush Alpine grass. Eventually, there is a car park and a trail that leads to the beautiful Bodensee, a small lake set at the end of the valley, fed by a cascading waterfall. A trout farm sits at the car park end of the lake, with a traditional wooden alpine restaurant off to the right. Doubtless fresh trout is their speciality! Decking juts out over the water, a scenic tableaux before you as you dine. The alm also boasts a menagerie to keep the children entertained; pigmy goats, llamas and chickens dwell side-by-side in noisy harmony. We often used to drive up there to walk the lake circuit. The far end crosses boggy marshes, as the stream wends from waterfall to lake. A wooden bridge provides the perfect vantage point for a rest and some photos. Plenty of benches line the trail for travellers like us to linger and savour the views, before inevitably treating ourselves to a hot chocolate and cake. Late afternoons would see us in the town. We'd park close to the Schaldminger Brewery, before choosing a hostelry to sample its wares. We were so happy in this wonderful part of the world. As we entered town there was the delightful Wintergarden café, where the outside tables had cosy blankets draped over the seats should the day turn chilly. Sometimes we would wander deeper into town, especially in the summer months, as there's a great walk alongside the foaming River Tabach. If we did the river walk around lunchtime, we would treat ourselves to your favourite, *Bratwurst mit brot,* at the sausage shack. In the main town hall car park, the little mobile kitchen did a steady trade. You had your sausage with mustard and ketchup, and I would have a schnitzel burger with a special sauce. We'd share a side of chips and sit on a bench with our 'black hats' on, watching the world go by. A bottle of Radler (shandy to us), washed it down, as good as any banquet.

We'd fly into Salzburg airport, which we loved; small, welcoming and very close to town, which made it an ideal stop over for a couple of nights before moving off to our chosen destination. Once we stayed in a 16th century hotel, with massive stone walls and little winding corridors. It poured with rain for the entire two days that time. Remember, I took a super photo of you sitting under an umbrella, a lager on the table, smiling of course, in your plum coloured waterproof. That now hangs on my photo wall, a daily reminder of that soggy visit. We stopped over there once with your mum, Jean, before going off to Schliersee in Bavaria for a week. That was June; warm and sunny thankfully, so we dragged your dear mum around all the sights, particularly those related to your beloved 'Sound of Music'. I think we forgot she was that much older than us. We quite exhausted her, but she loved it. If we had an early morning flight, we would often take a lingering, scenic journey to get to Schladming for a 3pm check-in. Remember the great lakes, Mondsee, Wolfgangsee, where we had a hearty goulash soup one wet arrival day? The lakes to the East of Salzburg were very tourist-orientated, but that afternoon in Mondsee is etched in our memories. We just had time for a sunny cruise on the lake. We got on and nabbed the two front seats in the bow; these didn't involve and stairs, and were easier for you. Then a coach party of chattering Japanese boarded and took over the whole upper deck. As the cruise started, the soundtrack to the Sound of Music came on, and the Orientals sang their hearts out. As did you, my darling, you were in your element!

33

TIME OUT

Just a quick round up of current events, my dear. Anna, who is handling the probate required by the NHS, blast their eyes (very apt!) informed me this week that the court were not happy with your will just being loose pages not in a binder. With a huge amount of restraint, I told Anna that it was all done online through McMillan in return for a donation, and printed off by me at home. As for putting it in a binder, I did have other things to occupy me at the time! As we know, my dear. Talk about jobsworths! I hate the hoops they are making me jump through, resurrecting memories of those horrible last few months. I'm coming to the end of my patience. I hope spring will give me a better outlook. I am so sorry, you deserve so much more.

I said to myself that I would use March to do some things around the flat. It's been a bit neglected, but then I rarely have visitors and I'm as happy as is possible. But I know you would not be pleased if I let Maisy (our Maisonette) become a typical 'old boys' place. So, new windows for the bedroom and kitchen are ordered, as the old ones are full of condensation. They should be fitted in April. I went straight for Rustington Windows, as the guy was so helpful when I called him in to see if we could get a front door that opened outwards to make getting off your stair lift easier. Alas, it was not to be. But that's why I've gone with them. If the weather ever improves, I have the leaking garage roof to sort out. I did toy with replacing it, but thought with some flashing tape and rust-proofing paint, it will probably see me out. I just hope I don't go through it when I get up there! Of course, the garden needs a lot of care and love, but I think I will enjoy that. I've got a new mesh to go over the pergola on the decking, to provide a bit of mottled shade should we actually get a summer. The seagulls have made a few holes in the present one, but if you recall we did use it as a camping ground sheet for a couple of years! Happy days... So I suppose we've had our money's worth out of it. Last week I fitted a new shower enclosure. As you know, after a while the seals and edges go mouldy and discoloured. I ordered one from Victoria Plum for £150. I was very impressed with it for the money, much better than our Wickes ones. Oh, but the fitting of it was a nightmare. The old side supports were so well stuck with silicone to the plastic shower boards they pulled great chunks out of them! And when I was carrying one of the old glass shower panels downstairs it touched the wall slightly... Whoosh! Five thousand glass crystals everywhere! What was really astounding, though, was that at the tip, when I threw the sister panel into the rubble skip, it didn't break! Finally, I got it all installed, but Bongle dear I have to say I'm surprised at how long it took me. I'm not the spritely DIYer I used to be! That came as a bit of a shock. So, I think it is right that I try and get our Maisy future-proofed while I am able.

It's now 22nd March, 2023, and I'm having a bit of a wobbly day emotionally. It's the AGM tonight for your dear WI, the Rusti-Belles. They'll award the Linda Coppard Trophy to this years most outstanding member. I know you would be so proud, as am I. In your words you would have been 'made up'!

Karen asked me if I would like to attend. I've been in such a quandary about what to do, as I know I'll just be a sobbing mess in the corner. After a lot of thought, I remembered that with the help of fellow member, Sandra, going to WI was one of the very few things you could do independently. You loved being able to do something girly, without hanging onto my arm and having me hovering in the background. So I've written a few words and a donation cheque for £500 – I know you would approve – and I've given it to Sandra to take tonight. I have been promised photos that I can share on Facebook. I'm writing this in the beach bar, sobbing over the tablet. Sarah has been chatting to me, cheering me up as I write; all the guys are so lovely down here.

The AGM went very well, my little script raised a laugh or two from the members, and I'm pleased to say your good friend Karen won your trophy in this first year. A super outcome, I know you'd be 'made up'!

Now I must write about somewhere really cheery, so it has to be Prien Am Chiemsee in Bavaria and Herr Wulf's wonderful Hotel Leopold Am See.

34

BAVARIA

What a hidden gem we found here, my darling! Few Brits ever get to see Chiemsee, to the south of Munich; a large body of fresh clean water from the mountains to the south, which also provide a superb backdrop. There's an island with one of mad King Ludwig's grand castles on it: *Neues Schloss Herrenchiemsee,* incorporating a copy of the hall of mirrors from the Palace of Versailles in France. There is also an abbey, a small community amidst beautiful, tree-lined walks – quite a magical place. Lake cruisers ply the waters, laden with tourists. King of these is the thundering paddle steamer 'Leo Fessler,' a sight to behold, with paddles foaming, pounding across the calm waters. Our favourites, though, were the small electric boats that could be hired from the quayside at Prien. They had one which was high-powered – the 'Schnell Boat,' they called it. I was a very happy boy when that was available!

The hotel sits overlooking the quayside where the lake steamers dock. Directly behind this is the station for what was once the goods line, going up into the small town of Stock, about a mile or so inland. Now the train, with it's vintage carriages, ferries tourists to and from the town and the main line station. There are just two hotel rooms that have a balcony, and we were always willing to pay extra as they overlooked the quayside and station. Do you remember that year your mum came with us? You would sit for hours together, watching the hustle and bustle.

We got to know the owner, Herr Wulf, quite well over the years. I did some nice reviews for him on various websites, and he rewarded us (your mother included), with a free dinner. What a charming gentleman! I had a Leger luxury coach tour brochure in the post this year, featuring that hotel as a stop over. I wonder if my reviews were an influence? The traditional-style restaurant was separate from the hotel, sitting diagonally opposite. It was fronted by a terrace, and had a large lawn filled with tables directly on the lakeside. From the lawn you could see straight across to the channel leading up to the waterside entrance of Herrenchiemsee Castle. From the dock, the gardens and fountains made the King's entrance quite spectacular. A few minutes away, on the picturesque Lakeside path, is a swimming complex that's quite innovative for its day. Lots of stainless steel spa areas, as well as a major pool that's both inside and outside. We've come across a few of these, and going from inside to a snow-covered wonderland while luxuriating in 30 degree water is an experience to remember! The spa at Prien had the crowning glory of this experience; stainless-steel bubbling spa beds at the edge of the pool. We laid on our tummies, heads pillowed on our arms, looking out at the lake and all manor of craft enjoying the waters. Oh, my darling Bongle, we haven't half done some wonderful things! The sad (or is it wonderful?) thing is, if not for writing this, those memories might never have seen the light of day. So I'll continue to remember, and write, even if it's only ever me that reads it all. Thank-you, my dear, for quite a special life.

We stayed at Herr Wulf's hotel on many occasions as a convenient stopover before, after or transiting a holiday resort. Being midway between Munich and Salzburg airports, it was ideally situated. It would often be around my birthday in April; asparagus, or 'spargel' season. We loved it – spargel soup, white spargel with hollandaise sauce, then lamb with tender green spargel... Vunderbar!

Do you recall Wasserburg, and the unique dining experience we enjoyed? We had an early evening flight out of Munich, so we decided to have a little explore across country on the way back and find somewhere for lunch. Wasserburg am Inn proved to be a delightful old walled town on an island in a loop of the river. Hence the name, I suppose: Water Town! We wandered the ancient streets and battlements, hand in hand as always... Oh, how I miss that touch. We found a place with outside tables that was very busy, always a good sign, and one table was free so we bagged it. There did not appear to be any waiting staff, and we saw people bringing out delicious looking plates of food, so in I went. There was a drinks counter, so first I got us two foaming steins of beer – got to get the priorities right! Looking around, it seemed to be self-service from several huge trays sitting under heat lamps. There were no menus, and no other clues, so I went back in and filled two plates with something I could recognise. In this case it was slow-cooked pork, practically falling apart and with the best crackling ever, plus cabbage, boiled potatoes and gloopy gravy to top it off. It was spectacularly good; we talked about it for years. We came to the conclusion it was some kind of community kitchen... I hope we qualified! The only downside of that trip was that your stupid husband left his favourite sunglasses on the café table in the airport, when we had a final Bavarian beer!

35
TIME OUT AGAIN

Well darling, I have returned from my birthday trip to Cornwall. This tablet has decided to delete the few pages I wrote while away, which sort of sets the scene for the trip; a bit of a disaster, and very, very lonely. The plus points were the scenery, and driving my wonderful new car. Yes, Bongle, yet another one! I'd best explain.

About three weeks ago, I was looking at campervans on Auto Trader, just for something to do. There was a 1990 Autohomes Kameo, the same model we took to Iberia after that horrible Hastings pub experience in 2000. The photos looked good, and at £9000 it was fairly cheap for nowadays. The guy was at university in Bath, and he could not have it there. He loved it, supposedly, but it had to go! His mum and dad were handling the sale, so off I trotted to Waterlooville. Well, the photos must have been taken years ago, and there was a bash on the high-top roof that had not been repaired, so the interior was damp and musty. It would be a full-blown restoration project. My hopes of recapturing the past and gaining a hobby were dashed, but probably for the best. That weekend I read an editorial in MMM, the Motorhome Magazine. The writer said things had changed since Covid; so many newbies who didn't follow the rules. As a result, many more councils have fitted height barriers and in some cases banned campers. The west coast of Scotland was particularly affected. So I thought, stop with the pipe-dream, you're not fit enough anyway! Then I thought, I love my Honda CRV, but it has two shortcomings: fuel consumption, and power. I remembered the blue HRV we had, and how it was a perfect size, but underpowered. Is the hybrid any better? I arranged a test drive, and wow, it drove beautifully and was much quicker than our one. But it was cramped and uncomfortable compared to my CRV. So I tested a CRV hybrid – brand new as it happens – and I adored it! Classy, fast and double the MPG of my Henry. It cost me a pretty penny, but it was only 11 months old, a dark, metallic blue. Henry was going to need new tyres and brakes this year, and was now six years old, although he'd only done 12,000 miles. I call the new one Evie – for electric vehicle, a common nickname I suspect. When I picked her up, two days before the Cornwall trip, I was astounded to learn that the first owner had intended to keep it for a while, and had paid for five years' extended warranty and servicing! A nice surprise, but tinged with sadness as it seems he got very ill. I suspect that bloody cancer... The car was too big for his wife, so, sad, but for once I got a result! And I love it. Driving Evie is now my number one pleasure. It might even help me to stop the damn wine!

ST MAWES, CORNWALL

Now to the holiday. I broke the journeys in Seaton again. Why do I do that? Even though it was still the Easter holidays, it was a ghost town. I had a wander in the cold and windy town, and decided to get a picnic from Tesco and retreat to the Premier Inn's comfy bed to watch the usual crap on TV. Next morning I queued for breakfast, but after watching the one poor girl on duty try to refill the coffee machine, top up cereals, seat people and answer questions, I gave up and settled for stopping on the way. It was pouring down, of course. Three hours to St Mawes; after an hour, I saw a National Trust sign for Castle Drogo. That sounded enticing, in a Hammer Horror sort of way, but below it was a sign for a guesthouse, café, and toilets! The latter are my nemesis when travelling; I often plot my routes via large supermarkets so I can have a pee. You're well aware of my obsession with not passing a gents loo, aren't you my dearest! Probably why the idea of a camper appeals so much... Now, if I could remove the passenger seat and put in a porta potti, it would be perfect! I visited the cafe and had the most lovely home-cooked full English breakfast. I'll remember that pit stop.

I got to St Mawes, and the weather was much more pleasant. I found my apartment easily, with a cracking view out over the boatyard, and down the estuary to St Andrew's Head. There was no sign of life, but the door was unlocked even though I was three hours early. I decided to put my food in the fridge, as it had been in the cool bag for 36 hours. Then I drove into town for a pint, to await check-in time. If that's a ten-minute walk to town, they must all be Olympians! It's a beautiful little town, with a picturesque harbour, narrow lanes leading up to the castle, and of course very expensive car parks! I paid £3 for two hours, and went to the Victory Inn for a lovely pint of Thatchers Gold cider. Returning to the boatyard, there was still no sign of life, so I moved in. It was a nice flat, but the furniture wasn't great. There were no drawers or baskets in the bedroom at all, so my socks and smalls stayed in the case. The lounge had two small sofas, but they were so soft and saggy it felt like my butt was on the floor. I had real trouble getting up from them, you would have found it hilarious! The views were superb, but in the evenings I just couldn't get comfortable on those sofas. Even piling up the cushions didn't help. On the opposite end of the scale, the bed was the firmest I have ever encountered. After a couple of days my back was killing me. I would go for long drives, to St Michael's Mount or Penzance, just to be comfortable in my lovely car. On Tuesday evening, with Wednesday being my birthday, I resolved to have a comfy bed for the night. I wanted to be waited on, so I booked Warners at Cricket St Thomas for my last two nights. On Wednesday morning I enjoyed the drive to Somerset, and as I was a bit early, I stopped off in Chard for a pint. Going back to the car, I saw hot pies in the butchers shop... I had steak and ale, great it was, and the sum-total of my dining out experiences on this trip. Well, except for that first days' breakfast. Getting to Warners I went to my room; oh yeah, comfy bed, tub chair, good shower... Heaven. At 7.30pm I wandered the quarter-mile to the restaurant, queued for a saddo-single table and read the menu. Argh! Wednesday, so it must be gammon! I endured it in silence. They've had the same damn menu for the last two years, that I know of. Happy Birthday to me! I got some texts, a couple of early cards to open, but no calls. The most lonely, miserable birthday I can remember. But at least the bed was comfy! On Thursday I endured a lonely breakfast and thought to myself, do I really want a repeat of yesterday? No. So I packed and ran for home... well, the beach bar actually, where the lovely Kat wished me Happy Birthday and bought me a pint! Why do I go away?

WOBBLE 4

I think that, in future, I'll go on road trips for the joy of driving, but only book the next day as I go. That way I can please myself day by day. The first two weeks of May have been very cold and wet. I decided to do some redecorating, as they made such a mess fitting the new windows in the bedroom and kitchen that it seemed the easiest way to make the rooms look good again. I have since found the right-hand bedroom window doesn't fit, and is a bugger to shut, but I can't bear to have those muppets in the house again. I wanted to get away from the beige look in the bedroom, although we did like it at the time, as it hid the tea and coffee spills! I thought it might wash away some of the images of that darned hospital bed in the lounge. I'm not sure you'd approve of my colour scheme, dearest, you were always the one with taste! The kitchen remains the nice light green we both liked, but the bedroom now has a plum-coloured wall behind the bedhead, with lilac walls. I think it works quite well. Of course, the paints aren't *called* plum and lilac, but that's what they are! The lounge proved more problematic. I thought the same plum colour would look good on the fireplace walls, but strangely, I thought pale yellow would go well on the remaining walls... It didn't. So I tried a bit of the light blue I'd bought for the bathroom. Argh! Awful. And the same morning, I'd knocked the toothbrush mug into the bathroom sink and cracked the bloody thing! Stop laughing, Linda, it's not funny! Anyway, looking at the corner where I hadn't experimented with colours, the original beige, or 'Whicker,' as it was called, looked pretty good. So off I went to Wickes in search of a pot of satin-finish in Whicker. Of course, like the adorable 'Pacific' in the bathroom, Whicker is no longer made. Only, it *is,* but now it's called 'Light Calico'! I made the mistake of looking at new vanity units as well, and ended up buying one based on the fact I could lift the box. But only just... My fitness is starting to concern me. Back in the garage, with no obvious way of opening the vanity unit box, I cut it open. Looking at the sink, it hit me: it's just big enough for a dibble of the hands, not a proper, useable bathroom sink. Damn, stop laughing, Linda! With the decorating finished and a sort of spring clean done as I went, the place doesn't look too bad. I did think that if (and it's a big if), the case for medical negligence is ever settled, I might renovate the whole place. Kitchen, bathroom, etc... But then I think, why? It works for me. Hardly anyone ever sees it, anyway. On the lawsuit though, I've had so much time to ponder, and all sorts of things go through my mind. There has never been any mention of criminal proceedings, corporate manslaughter, death by neglect... Hell, just plain murder! But I must try to suppress these thoughts. By God though, it's not fair. Why you, my dear, sweet, kind, Linda?

I'm looking forward to my Baltic cruise in June, on the small, adults-only Arcadia. It seems like a long time since I actually had an enjoyable break. I hope it lives up to expectations. I'm looking forward to having proper time to write, and for learning how to use my super new camera. Norway, Sweden, Denmark, Poland and Germany; there should be some great photo opportunities. I've given up all hope of losing weight in three weeks. I just have no incentive to stop drinking. Hell, I even looked at Dignitas in Switzerland yesterday, but you have to be terminally ill before they put you to sleep – not just a fat, depressed alcoholic! So, Bongle, I bought some more 5XL shirts and two pairs of 48 inch trousers. Bloody hell! My decreasing mobility does worry me. With the weather slowly improving, I should be a lot more active. I plan to get on the bike early tomorrow, before doing my food bank run to the Witterings. I'll put the teak oil in the saddle bags, and give your memorial bench slat and your neighbours a bit of a shine. The inscription reads, 'Linda Jayne Coppard, she loved to 'walk the line.' RIP darling.' I often sit by it, on the prom in Littlehampton, and talk to you.

I had a bit of a moment yesterday. I'm trying to have a clear out; there's so much stuff in the garage and sheds, it will be a nightmare for whoever comes after me. Our Christmas decoration box was in the firing line. I'll never put any up again, so I'll see if your sister wants any of the nicer pieces. My dear, when I opened the box, laying on top were the Father Christmas, trees and gold trinket box we made together just before your diagnosis. That was it, the floodgates opened. They were self-assembly wooden kits from The Works; I put them together and you painted them. I can picture it now, you hunched over your crafting table, happy as can be. You'd just finished making all our Christmas cards as well. I did eventually send them a year later… It would have been a crime not too. Enough! I can't handle this.

Most of the decorations will go to the tip, but I think now that I'm over the shock, those two enchanting items can live in the summerhouse with all our other memories. Remember darling, how I put all our photographs that were on CDs onto a hard drive, so they would be safe forever? I'm so pleased that we looked at all ten years' worth in the weeks before you went into hospital. I have been trying to access the drive to put the odd memory on Facebook now and again. Strangely, it doesn't open on any of the computers or even the TV. Are you trying to tell me not to dwell in the past? I doubt anyone would have tried to view them, but I'll leave a note in the box just in case.

The garden is starting to come together. Many of our plants didn't survive the winter, including your beloved Hot Lip Salvias. But don't panic! I got some more from Ferring Nurseries, along with another ten shrubby things. I really notice my fitness decline while gardening; I have to sit down every thirty minutes or so. But slowly, it's all coming together. All we need now is sunshine and warmth. May is turning dry, but there's a constant chilly north wind, something to do with the Jet Stream being off-kilter. I've fixed the leaks in the garage roof, so that will see me out now, and hopefully so will the new fence. Andy's rose, Simply the Best, is shooting up, well in advance of the others. Must be its Scottish heritage!

I'm really looking forward to the Baltic cruise on the 6th June. I hope it will enable me to pull myself together, and come to terms with life just being me – not an 'us' anymore. It's horrible. I had a moment of panic when the '3 weeks to go' self-check-in email arrived, and I realised I hadn't booked the included port car park. The website was saying no availability. I'd normally have done it just after booking, I am definitely slipping! I rang the parking company, pleading decrepitness, and said I might not go if I had to struggle with cases on the train. Bless him, he got me booked in. If there is a next time, I'll book it straightaway. I guess it could be busy, as it is D-Day, and there might be some short anniversary cruises to Normandy. Anyhow, all sorted, so I just need to pack ready for a child-free holiday. Bliss! No dogs, either – I can't believe how badly behaved some dogs are in the beach bar, and the owners just ignore the black looks from other patrons. It's becoming – no, it *is* – a bloody selfish, me, me, me world. I won't miss it, when the time comes.

I had lunch with Chris, Olwyn, Kathy and Bruce yesterday at The Thatched Inn in Keymer. Chris wanted a ride in the new car; as usual, the drive from home to the back end of Brighton was a nightmare, but I think Chris enjoyed it. He's still very poorly and needs another operation. In many ways he is like you, and I can imagine him saying, "Why me?" As if being blind is not enough bad luck in life... But he and Olwyn seem to make the best of things. I mentioned that I'd been researching Dignitas in Switzerland at the weekend, thinking it might prompt a conversation about my depression. It didn't; they just said, 'don't be silly'. I said that if I get ill and start loosing mobility, there's nobody to look after me, so choices need to be made before getting too far down the line. The silence was deafening. Last night I realised that I'm on my own, and can only worry about me going forward. All the more reason for me to buck my ideas up, lose weight and get fitter... The trouble is, what's the bloody incentive? The court case drags on... Now that would be a morale boost, if it's ever concluded. It would allow me to plan at least, but I won't hold my breath. I miss you, darling.

You know Bongle, over the years we've had all manner of adventurous holidays, from road trips to France and Spain, Germany and wonderful Austria, to Alpine great railway journeys. And not forgetting our camping trips, be it in campervans, the motorhome and finally caravans… We saw some wonderful sights, from an age where borders and currencies still existed. It's a testament to our compatibility that living in such close proximity, sometimes for weeks on end, never caused us any major falling out. It's all the harder, now, to find any satisfaction.

38

CHARLIE GOES TO SPAIN

Enough of the doom and gloom of modern life! Time to relive another of our glorious trips... But where? How about the three week road trip to the Costa Del Sol in Charlie? Oh, how we loved that car! We bought your mum's Mazda 323 when she got a new Citroën C3. It was lilac, low mileage and economical, but no fun whatsoever. After a few months – I'm guessing this was around 1996, our golden years for adventure – I spotted Charlie in Portland Carriage Company, close to our flat in Hove. An F-registration, white, two-door VW Golf Mk2. Gti, F50 CHC, hence 'Charlie Coppard'... it was fate. I remember picking you up from your job at the Legal Aid Board in Brighton and trying to talk you into seeing it. Of course, Bongle, you had your sensible head on and said 'NO!' But when you saw him, you were smitten too, and it was more or less a straight swap for your mum's low mileage, much newer car. Although I don't think she was too happy! So we gained a Charlie. Boy was he fun; powerful, with great handling; a road trip was definitely called for. I was working as a mechanic at the TA centre back then, so taking it in to the workshop at weekends was not a problem. A full service, new brake pads and lots of polishing later, we had a real grand tourer ready to go.

To keep the costs down a bit, we took our small tent and gas stove. We were fit back then, camping when possible on the outward and home trips. Holiday and breakdown insurances were bought, maps studied – no Google back then, or even mobile phones – ferries booked, and we were off!

We got the overnight ferry from Portsmouth to Caen, choosing the hellish reclining seats to save the cost of a cabin – a mistake we would not repeat in future trips!

A long driving day later found us pitching the tent in a small campsite in Souillac, on the banks of the river Dordogne. We strolled into town and had a couple of beers and an unmemorable meal. After that, we watched a group of canoeists beating up and down the river, practicing capsizing manoeuvres and generally having a great time. Tiredness drove us into the tent as soon as it was dark; I hoped for an early start so we could be in Spain the next day. Around 1am the rain came. Heavy, noisy thundering rain, which kept us from sleeping and turned the grass of the campsite into a quagmire.

As soon as it was light, we broke camp in the rain and loaded up Charlie. Breakfast could wait until we'd dried out a bit. The sopping wet tent was laid on top of the luggage, hopefully to try and dry out; the car windows immediately misted up, so we sat there warming the engine until the windscreen cleared. We had fun getting onto firm ground, slipping and sliding all over the place... We laughed afterwards, but not for a while!

We headed off up a long, steep hill, paused at the patisserie to get some hot fresh croissants, and drove off into the rising sun. An hour later, when the day had some warmth, we stopped and opened the tailgate to let the steaming boot dry out. We then feasted on English tea with French croissants atop a high hill, enjoying stunning views of the Dordogne valley. It was magical!

We hit the toll motorways to get a few miles in by lunchtime. They may be expensive, but with a picnic stop or full service station every ten kilometres, they're wonderful to use. Charlie was in her element, and chewed up the miles. We took the A61 to Narbonne, the ancient walled city of Carcassone flashing past in the distance. Lunchtime found us on the A9, with Perpignan coming up and the border just beyond. I wanted to get past Barcelona before stopping; that way we'd have most of the big driving days behind us, and would be able to enjoy the journey. Oh darling, if only that were to be true!

We stayed on the motorway, breaking at the border to spend our first Pesetas – no Euros yet – on fuel and strong coffee. On we drove, signs for alluring places whizzing by; L'Escala, Pallafrugell, Tossa de Mar and Blanes... The whole of the beautiful Costa Brava was lost behind us.

Barcelona was as a hazy mass in the distance as we took the bypass; around 4pm we drove through the centre of Salou, a very touristy coastal town on the Costa Dorada. I saw a sign for a campsite, and followed it across the railway line and up a small but steep hill. We booked in and found a nice spot, enclosed by shrubs. We set up camp and started to explore our surroundings. As usual, the swimming pool was filled with local kids, so we headed down to the beach and the promenade for a well-deserved relax.

There was a lovely paved walkway, with the beach on one side. The other side was lined with hotels and cafés, selling all manner of British food: pies, burgers and of course chips with everything. It was a bit late for a swim, so we had a couple of beers and put the old 'black hats' on. It was a great place for people watching. Hours can be spent observing the English package tourist at play, and there is never a dull moment! We used to guess where they came from, based on their clothes. It was easy to spot the campers, as opposed to hotel tourists – like us, the campers were normally of a slightly creased appearance!

Back at the site, we had new neighbours; two teenage couples, also with a white VW Golf. They eyed the Gti with envy, and we felt quite proud of our Charlie.

After a shower, we headed back to the seafront, seeking a more traditional Spanish meal. We walked away from Salou and its pies, in the direction of Cambrils de Mar. We both enjoyed a wonderful fish dinner in a nice, peaceful restaurant; your favourite, Lin, mixed fried fish, and me with my favourite, pan-fried Dover Sole. A stroll along the prom towards the bright lights and noise of Salou helped to set us up for a final bottle of wine in one of the beachfront bars.

Next day, a gentle drive to Benidorm was all we had planned. We got there at around 11am, to find a heaving mass of humanity. After eventually finding a parking space, we had an English breakfast, and for my sins I had a pint of beer. You had a coffee, wise girl. Then we set off to find a hotel for the night, or possibly two. No chance! Not a room was to be had in Benidorm. We went to the old town and walked for miles, but nothing was available.

Setting off in Charlie, with no real thought of where to try next, we hit the motorway. As we settled into the drive, stereo playing, I seemed to be on autopilot to the Costa del Sol. You dozed most of the way. I didn't think how tedious it must have been for you, but you never complained, darling. Perhaps you should have, more often. I get these thoughts now and then, that can never be answered. Were you really happy? Or was it just a case of letting me get on with it? I would give a lot now to have your guiding wisdom. I make so many mistakes in my impetuous haste.

It was 8pm when we rolled, exhausted, into Nerja. 600 miles, not all dual carriageways either, in one horrendous day! Worse – I had driven by many wonderful places on the Costa Blanca, silly sod. You said if I ever put you through a hell like that again, you would get a divorce… After having castrated me with a blunt knife! I hadn't really thought it through. It must have been that breakfast pint! It was a hell of a long way, and with the sun coming in through your side window all afternoon, you got fried! I am so sorry, my darling, and things like this haunt me now as I can't ask you if you forgive me. Of course, the hostel we had visited in the past, and loved, was full. It was getting late; all I could find was a six-bed apartment for the night, at the price of three nights in the hostel Marazul. Idiot!

Next morning we, walked down to the Marazul. They said they were full, but could have a room the next day. However, it was first-come, first-served. We decided to come back the following day, at breakfast, and tonight we would use the out of town campsite. A nice swim in the clear waters of the Mediterranean refreshed us, and after that we moved out of the apartment and headed for the campsite. It was up in the hills, close to the famous caves of Nerja. There was a pool and a small shop, but it was as hot as Hades itself. I would have to redeem myself somehow!

The hostel remained full. Of course it would, being on the seafront and very reasonable, complete with air conditioning! But I had an idea... A good one, I hoped.

A short phone call later and we were on our way, to Bena Vista! I'd been able to pay for an extra three nights in our apartment, so we could check in straight away! Luxury at last.

Darling, the script on this grand tour was copy-and-pasted from the last chapter of Two Clots in a Camper, written long ago. Obviously, I've had to edit it. Mainly (and awfully), to put you in the past tense. But it has made me realise what a prat I was, even with your calming influence. I think as I grow older, more grumpy and frankly more stupid, there is little hope for me. Reliving these adventures with you, my dearest, is about as good as it gets.

On the two-hour drive, we perked up considerably. After being homeless, the comfort of our timeshare apartment would be fantastic. For those of you who have never experienced this type of property, I'll give you an idea what it's like. The best thing is that most are of 4-star quality or above, so you know you will have a good apartment. We always have, anyway.

Our complex is built in the Andalusian white village style, little three-storey blocks of whitewashed apartments clad in Bougainvillea. Flowerbeds line the paths between the terraces. They're all named after star signs; our complex, Sagittarius, has its own heated pool in a walled garden, with sun loungers all around. We're on the first floor, a one-bedroom apartment with a south-facing balcony. There are twin beds and a ceiling fan in the bedroom, marble floors throughout, a small but fully-equipped kitchen that has an archway into the dinning area, and a table for four all laid up, with complimentary wine in the middle. The passage to the bedroom has a marble-tiled bathroom leading off it. The dining area has three steps down to the lounge level, a sofa/bed, two armchairs, satellite TV, video player, stereo, fans and heaters, and a glass coffee table. French windows lead on to the balcony where a table, four cushioned chairs and a barbeque complete the picture.

The whole complex has an adjacent commercial centre with a great mixture of shops and a variety of good restaurants, plus a lawn bowls rink and tennis courts. All this within five minutes walk of our room! The only drawback is that it's situated on the side of the busy main coast road. With the beach also a stone's throw away, we loved it – obviously, that's why we bought a second week in August! We made full use of our weeks didn't we darling, banking them and exchanging them for beautiful places all over Europe. Timeshare really worked for us.

So it was with great joy that we dumped our bags on the cool marble floor and left the apartment. We only had an hour until the shops closed for their long lunch break and siesta. We were sad to find that Dave, our old friend and the resort manager from our previous visit, had left the company. We never did find out why, or see him again.

We drove to Estepona and our favourite Hypermarket; we need essential supplies, mainly soft drinks, beer, wine and a bottle of Brandy to mix with chocolate milk to produce a nightcap called La Mumbas. Ham, cheese, biscuits, water, cakes and other essential supplies were thrown into the trolley to see us through the next ten days.

Back on our sun-drenched balcony we opened a warm beer each, and with a bowl of plain crisps and a jar of olives, we sat back and savoured the luxury of having our very own space. We sat out there and read until the sun went down; it was the first real chance we'd had to enjoy some peaceful sunbathing since we left home. You were in your element at last, Bongle.

We stayed in the area most evenings, trying the different menus; one of the Chinese restaurants did the most wonderful crispy duck with pancakes and plum sauce. It was quite an experience watching the young but skilled waiter taking all the meat off the bone for us at the table. Afterwards, at Rory's Irish Bar, they would often have live music, and the owner joining in with his bagpipes!

The area we were in provided plenty of choices for days out. We were situated halfway between Marbella to the east and Estepona to the west. Marbella, with its millionaire's playground of a harbour, is always a grand source of entertainment for serious people watching. It also boasts the Court del Ingles, a mega shopping complex, as well as a lovely old town centre, with the fabulous Orange Square as the focal point. Estepona, by contrast, is much more our sort of town; a more down-to-earth marina, with affordable bars and a good assortment of restaurants. The port boasts a tourist market on Sunday mornings, but the proper Wednesday market in the town centre is a must-see full of everyday items. We always restocked with dried herbs, and got yet another wall plate or lantern to hang on the outside walls of our garden at home... Some of them survive to this day.

There's a nice beach and promenade to stroll along in Estepona, with charming little wooden cafés on the prom. It's fascinating to sit with a beer and watch the cook turn out meals in seconds for the workers who pop in for lunch. Surprisingly, she spoke to us in a broad Yorkshire accent. Having married a Spanish gentleman some years before, it was wonderful to hear her switch languages without even blinking. It put us to shame! We had some wonderful times didn't we, Lin. But we should still be having many more.

A hour to the north of our apartment is the ancient town of Rhonda. Spanning a deep gorge is a historic and beautiful 18th century bridge, the views from which are amazing. The bullring is also a famous attraction of the town; inaugurated in 1785, it's thought by many to be the spiritual home of bullfighting. Interesting shops and enticing café's fill the narrow streets... it's well worth the trip. I should point out though, that some folk find the winding road up to Rhonda a bit traumatic. We loved it, and so did our Charlie.

These visits filled our daylight hours, with every other day finding us lounging around the pool, reading and soaking up the sunshine. The cool of dusk allowed us to cross the footbridge over the main road and explore further afield; new bars, or a different stretch of beach on every walk. We would usually return to our own patch to dine, not wanting to be too far from home should we have one drink too many. Or, as sometimes happens, urgently needing our own bathroom!

The days flew by, and all too soon it was time to bid farewell to Bena Vista. We were undecided as to which way to head home. Should we take the quickest route, up through Spain's centre then along the north coast to France, or go back the way we'd come? Being well-rested, we decided to start early on the Saturday morning, have a long driving day, and see if we could get to the Alicante area in one hit. If we went on the motorways that cut off the corner by Almeria, it should be a lot quicker than that dreadful 600-mile day coming down.

By evening we had a comfortable room in a seafront three-star hotel in Altea, which is Benidorm's more authentic neighbour. All thoughts of camping were long forgotten! That evening, we strolled along the newly-constructed promenade, the glare of Benidorm in the distance, and found a restaurant on the seafront. I can't remember the meal, but I do recall the friendly Dutch manager, who told us: "The Spanish are not so silly! They give Benidorm to the English, and save Altea for themselves. A good arrangement, yes?" We had to agree.

It was a very pleasing, surprisingly unspoilt place.

Do you remember, dear, on the Sunday, we saw crowds gathering on the beach and street outside the hotel? We were about to witness a charming event; the blessing of the sea, and the local fishermen. A priest stood on the beach while a small fishing boat headed for shore with a statue of the local patron saint on the deck, garlanded with flowers. A band played, the priest preached, and the saint was hoisted aloft by the crowd and paraded up and down the street. We viewed all this from the balcony at the end of the first-floor corridor. Another British couple joined us, I fetched some cold beers from our room, and we all enjoyed the spectacle.

Our new friends were ex-pats, who lived in Mojacar, a few hours down the coast. They loved to escape to Altea for a break every now and then. They told us they ran a business cleaning and maintaining holiday homes for owners who were away or renting them out; we felt quite envious. That evening we dined with them, their local knowledge taking us to a little workman's café where we had a very cheap and tasty meal. Unfortunately, we also drank a lot of very cheap wine, beer and brandy, making us definitely a little the worse for wear. It's all a bit hazy, but suffice to say I was glad we only had a relatively short drive the next day. We did enjoy the company, though.

Blanes, just North of Barcelona, was where we fetched up. It looked quite wonderful, so we decided to stop here for three nights before the long trip back through France. It was early afternoon when we parked on the picturesque seafront, a golden sandy beach filled with sunbathers and swimmers right in front of us. I was looking forward to a good swim next day, though you weren't keen on sea-bathing.

We walked past all the seafront hotels, hoping for a room similarly priced to Altea. Not likely! This was a much more touristic and pricey place.

One street back though, we found a nice hotel with a car park run by a friendly lady called Anna. We were immediately welcomed and made to feel at home. Anna's husband showed us to our room; we later found out he was a biochemist for a big multi-national company, and only occasionally helped out in the hotel. A small British tour company also used the hotel. Some of their guests had been returning to Anna's for years, and we could see why. We stayed there twice in all, before they sold up and retired; such a shame, as we felt quite at home there.

After a reviving siesta, we enjoyed an evening walk along the seafront. At the northern end of the prom is the fishing port, very much a working harbour. Tree-lined gardens are filled with tables and chairs. Nimble waiters dodge the traffic of the coast road to deliver laden trays to hungry diners from their establishments on the 'wrong' side of the street. Above the port, perched on the cliffs are the botanical gardens, which we planned to see the next day. The southern end of town was a busy area, with the main package tour hotels and plenty of camping sites, right on the beach. If only we'd seen them on our last trip, in the camper van, we would have stayed a week or two!

Opposite Anna's hotel there was a café. Just an ordinary little corner eatery, with plastic tablecloths and a large window that opened onto the street. Stools placed on the pavement invited us to have a beer while deciding what to do about dinner. Our budget was being severely stretched by not camping, but no way were we going back to that tent. Sitting there, perched overlooking the serving area, it occurred to us what a charming little place we'd found. The husband was manning the beer pump, his wife cooking and their daughter serving. The owner chatted to us as best he could; we answered as best we could, all parties gesticulating wildly to add meaning to our often-wrong linguistic attempts. It was such fun!

The food looked superb. People came and ate in a constant stream; a regular turnover of customers suggested it had to be good, and the prices on the menu board were very, very reasonable. We moved inside to a table in the corner, where we could observe our fellow diners. There were quite a few things on offer that we'd need our phrase book to decipher, but since we'd left it four storeys away in the room, we settled on a saffron rice and chicken special. With an earthenware jug of the local wine, we devoured a tasty feast. Then we blew the budget by having two La Mumbas each… What the hell, we were having a great time! So for the second night in a row, we fell into bed in an alcoholic daze.

Next morning, after two cups of Anna's strongest coffee and a big jug of cold water, we felt ready to explore the botanical gardens. They were designed in 1928 and boast over 7,000 species of Mediterranean and tropical plants. We didn't fancy the long slog up the steep road to the entrance. Fortunately, passing through town we'd noticed a curious contraption plastered with the garden name, darting about picking up people. The vehicle we flagged down was like a miniature articulated lorry, the open back of its trailer filled with hard wooden seats. The maniac driver whizzed through the narrow back streets and then onto the hairpin bends leading up the cliff – hence the need to be articulated. I hoped we wouldn't meet any poor unfortunates who might be walking down the hill!

A good couple of hours were spent strolling through the magnificent borders, in part overlooking sheer cliffs onto rocky beaches. Exotic flora abounded as we wound around the rocky paths. It was quite hot – very hot, actually, and a drink was becoming a priority, so we braved the road and walked down to the port for a cold drink. Fanta lemon for a change, it was very welcome indeed.

I was determined to swim on this great beach. Loaded down with all the usual beach gear, towels, books, snack, drinks, flippers and snorkel (twit!) we laid on the sands facing the crashing waves. Well, it wasn't sand really, more like small gravel, which is much nicer as it doesn't get into all the awkward places like sand does. Or so I thought... You, Bongle, would be content to lay on the beach and watch your idiot husband thrash about in the surf.

It was scorching hot, but with a stiff wind blowing, the urge to swim soon overtook me. Lin, you wisely elected to stay on the beach. I should have asked myself why nobody else was in the water; some people were just sitting in the sand, letting the surge wash over their legs, but not me. Oh no, I run straight in! Whoosh, the wave swept my legs from under me. I was on my butt, waves crashing over me, the undertow trying to drag me out to the depths. Panic set in as I scrabbled to regain my footing; luckily, a big wave slammed me in the back and sent me sprawling to the relative safety of the shallows. As I staggered back towards our spot, you were laughing fit to burst! I felt like my swimming shorts didn't feel quite right... I'd accumulated a couple of pounds of gravel in the crotch of my sagging swimwear, and they were slowly en route to my knees! Sheepishly, I bailed out the stones, while an orange-clad lifeguard bawled at me in Spanish. He pointed to a huge red flag, directly behind where you lay on the beach... Whoops!

Next day, there was a strange feeling about the town. It seemed like a Sunday; the shops were closed, flags adorned tooting cars, and people were greeting each other with shouts of Viva Catalonia! It was September the 11th, and a very jolly day it was, too. In the hotel, Anna passed out cakes and pastries to everyone in sight, telling us it was a tradition on Catalonia Day. Lunchtime saw a very dapper gentleman patronising the hotel bar; he insisted on buying drinks for everyone, refusing any attempt to buy him one back. A friendly and proud race, the Catalans. We felt very at home there.

Even the small group of Russian tourists who also stayed at Anna's joined in the free eating and drinking. They usually kept themselves very much to themselves. They were a long way from home, we had wondered how all this must seem to them after the austerity of Moscow at that time. We wondered also if there was one central place in Russia that sold all the out-dated summer wear from the West, as they all seemed to be wearing near-identical clothes from about ten years before. If you could get one of them to speak to you, they seemed to be friendly, and were having a great time on holiday. The downside of the special day was that very few restaurants were open that evening, it being a big family holiday. Instead, we snacked on bar nibbles and crisps. We regretted only being able to stay in Blanes for such a short time, but we'd pushed our stay to the limits. We now only had two days to cover 800 miles back to Caen. But we vowed that would return... And we did!

8.30am saw us crossing the border back into France, and powering up on our return route. We refilled with cheaper Spanish petrol at the border, sank our last cheap coffee, and resigned ourselves to a day in the car. The journey was largely uneventful. Keeping to the 120kph limit of the motorways, every now and again some idiot would come screaming past at ridiculous rate of knots. One such fool we saw ten minutes later, his distinctive car piled, literally, up against a concrete slip-road divider. A police car was in attendance, no doubt awaiting the ambulance and body bag. It never fails to amaze me how Europeans, the French in particular, get so much speed out of their cars. Invariably they have the basic, small engine economy model, or foul-smoking, rattling diesels, yet they go like the blazes. If they ever all got fast cars, I think they'd destroy themselves in minutes.

By 5pm, we were sick and tired of sitting in the car. I was very conscious of not subjecting you to another long driving day, dearest, so we found a village off the main road. I can't remember exactly where, except it had 'Argetan' in its name – but then, a lot of rural French villages do! There was a nice little hotel, the sort with rickety-floored rooms, and ancient feather beds that you positively sink into. We went for a stroll by the river, followed by a couple of glasses of local red wine in a little Tabac.

With no sign of any other restaurants, we ate in the hotel. The friendly but unilingual waitress tried to explain the menu. One of the dishes seemed to be turkey; playing safe, we ordered that. It turned out to be a turkey drumstick each, with vegetables! Strange. Then I committed a cardinal sin – one that you remembered for years! I ordered two brandies to go with our coffees. The waitress said, "Cognacs?" I said, "Yes please!" I thought that would round off the day nicely. I didn't realise that they take these things seriously in France; particularly here, as we were in the heart of Cognac country! Those two drinks cost more than the ruddy room!

The next day, we made the ferry home without incident. We'd enjoyed the trip and learned a few things as well. I suspect, Linda, that you already knew the lessons. We'd passed so many beautiful places on Costas that we had never visited in my – yes, *my* – haste to reach somewhere familiar. Damn silly!

WOBBLE 5

A quick update on your negligence case, darling. Six weeks ago I gave permission for them to view my medical records, supposedly to see how long I'm likely to live. Not long, while this drags on! The doctors are concerned about my depression, mainly caused by missing you, and not being able to move on until this case is finished. Ironically, as of yesterday, my surgery have not released the records! I have an appointment with the doctor after yet another of these endless Bank Holidays, so I'll try to find out what is happening. The NHS Trust admitted failing to save you two years ago, so if they think they're doing the NHS a favour they're wrong! Having killed you, they're now doing their best to finish me off. It was *eight weeks* after the request that they finally released the records. Argh!

So I've decided, to hell with it! I have enough money left for another non-frugal twelve months. After that, do I really care? So I've booked another cruise... I know, crazy! My Tuesday drinking buddy, Roy, has a step daughter who works for Travel Village, the company we booked our first few cruises with. Roy told her about me, and last week she sent through some 'No solo surcharge' offers – one being for a sixteen-night trip around Iceland in September. The ship is Arcadia, it's adults-only, and two lovely people I met last year have already booked it. It's under a £100 a night, with parking and spends, so I booked it. I know it was always on our wish list, but one of us will see it and I will talk you through every step. Sadly, I doubt I'll feel comfortable enough with my weight, or this damn hernia, to swim in the Blue Lagoon. I'm in a bit of a state my dear; my mobility is worsening, and my weight is not going down. I'm still drinking, damn it, but it gets me through each day. I always was my own worst enemy.

Not long now till my Baltic cruise, and I'm hoping it will be a good one. Meanwhile I've been busy in the garden; I have a mission to keep it up to scratch, as befits your memory and all the happy hours we spent looking out on it from the summerhouse. There was an invasion of ants inside the summer house, as I discovered when itching like crazy after sitting in there for twenty minutes! I stripped it all out, lifted the matting and vacuumed thoroughly. Then I creosoted the wood floor. It's a bit stinky for now, but I think it will keep them at bay. The borders, and your memorial rose bed, are on the verge of being quite spectacular. I'll be putting some pictures on Facebook when it's at its best. I got six more roses from Ferring Nurseries; one is a pale blue, in an old English rose style, you would have loved it, darling. It's still hard to believe I can never share the garden with you again… Except perhaps, in time our ashes will merge here. It's June the 2nd tomorrow, our 33rd anniversary. It will be a tough day, so I've got to keep busy. I'll be shopping for the old dears, Betty and Patricia. I've warned them it needs to be three weeks' worth, so that will take a couple of hours. Then back to the garden. I'm halfway through replacing the mesh shading I put on the gazebo to keep the sun off your delicate skin. The seagulls finally made a few holes in the old one, but it lasted for two years. I do wonder if I shall be fit enough, or even here in two years' time to replace it again.

Now it's time to lighten up with another of our wonderful travel adventures. But which one?

DIEPPE, NORMANDY (OR FRANCE, FOR MY AMERICAN READERS!)

We've visited this French port many times, for short breaks and as a jumping off point for many other trips and tours. Back in the pre-Eurozone days, the 'booze cruise' was another great reason for going. The excellent Hypermarket provided us with great beers, wines, cheeses and Normandy cider. Over the years we've bought many things; you'll remember the delicate dinner service, white with silver rings. I've still got a couple of pieces even now, Bongle. From the town centre shops, the four plaster circus figures that reside to this day on the shelf halfway up the stairs. Even now, when I wash them I can remember us buying them; the shopkeeper wrapped them in newspaper for us. Then there's the extravagant painting we fell in love with; it cost about £50, a fortune to us twenty-five years ago, but it was so lovely. It's faded now, but still in the hallway. The view of a Mediterranean hillside, lavender clad, leading into a whitewashed village then on to the small cove with a sailboat anchored. When it was above the fireplace in our bungalow, how many times did we imagine ourselves walking that path to the shoreline? Memories baby. That's all there is now.

From Dieppe we had several trips along that chalky coast. Fécamp was a favourite; we stayed in the rooms above Le Frigate restaurant, room 2 having a sea view. In the daytime we visited the grand Palais de Benadictine, where the liqueur is made. An overpowering scent of dried herbs came from the huge bins where the ingredients were stored, ready to be mixed. We really enjoyed that tour, the building was beautiful, and then of course there was the tasting! But for you, my fish loving wife, the highlight was discovering the dish called 'Marmite'. A mound of rice surrounded by fish, prawns and mussels in a creamy sauce, with crisp fresh French bread... Superb! Linda, you must remember that weekend in Dieppe we took one year in December. We stayed in one of the nice big chain hotels, Accor, I think, on the seafront, overlooking the lawns and the beach. The room had a sea view; behind the bedhead was a false wall with an open plan bathroom behind it, which was quite strange. The cosy bar had alcoves lined with book shelves, it was a bit like drinking in a library! But our favourite venue was in the centre of town, a very old establishment called Cafe Des Tribunaux. Wood and glass panels lined the walls, and a mezzanine level looked down on the huge art-deco white-glass-bowl lampshades and the customers below. Newspapers mounted on wooden rods were provided for the patrons, stored at the feet of numerous bronze statues on plinths; it was like going back a hundred years! We spent many hours sitting with our black hats on, people watching, enjoying a bottle of wine. Sometimes two!

The evenings would see us strolling the short walk to the harbour side. The restaurant Newhaven was our regular haunt; invariably we would have Moules et Frites, our favourite. Before I met you, darling, I would never have dreamt of eating a mussel... Hell, I didn't even like tomatoes! The trip inevitably ended with a run to the Hypermarket to stock up on wine... We had some great little forays there, over the years.

41

THE BALTIC ON ARCADIA

Well, another cruise darling... Probably another disaster. Why do I keep doing it? Yesterday started well enough. Staggered boarding so no waiting; I breezed through, though it was too late for lunch. It's a comfortable cabin, much the same as our favourite on the Ventura – even a mini bath! You might just have fitted, but no chance for me. The shower-on-a-hose is a plus though, even if it is a bit weak. I mostly eat in the buffet, as the thought of dining with a group of strangers fills me with dread. For some unknown (and very stupid) reason, P&O have decided to remove all the serving trays from their buffets, on all the ships! Unbelievable. You remember how I used to get both of our meals for us? Can't be done now. It means you have to visit the counters multiple times, and risk loosing your table every time. Sadly, this will occupy my thoughts for much of this trip – stupid for stupid's sake. I'm going put a tray in my luggage next time! Speaking of stupidity, this is the same ship I'll be on for Iceland in September. I do wonder if I can bring myself to enjoy it. We always wanted to swim in the Blue Lagoon; impossible, the size and shape I am now... Perhaps that's the incentive I need to stop drinking and loose weight? But I still don't really want to be here without you.

The ship itself is quite different from the other ones we've been on; smaller, adults-only, and built as a liner, rather than a cruise ship. There aren't as many entertainment areas and you can see it's designed for travelling the larger oceans with rougher seas. The exterior is not as accessible as our favourite, Ventura. There's two-and-a-half sea days to Alesund in Norway. I think the time will weigh heavily, although I did sleep soundly through till 7am. Of course, I went to the casino last night; £100 down already! But even that is becoming boring. I'm not even sure if I'll go to bingo this afternoon. I'm writing in the Crows Nest bar, in the bow just below the bridge. The bar is the only table high enough for writing; it's a moulded circular bar, but with a damned lip on the edge that digs into my arm when writing. I'll have to try and find a more comfortable spot, but I suspect it may end up being the cabin. At least I'm doing a lot of walking while finding my way around. You would have hated me dragging you all over the place while I found my way. After a month of solid sunshine at home, it's strange to encounter the grey and gloomy North Sea. Today, 8th June, would have been your 68th birthday. It's going to be hard to get through. I went for breakfast at 9am, but not a table to be had. I just had some cereal standing up; had there been trays, I might have got two courses and hunted for a table. I attended a lecture in the theatre at 11.15 again; yesterday's was on the railways of the first World War, and today's was on the Fjords. I left my damn hearing aids in the cabin, twit! Then I found a small table in the pub where I am now writing. It's the right height! Ten minutes after I sat down, the place filled up. I'm now sitting here in the middle of the quiz we loved, which used to be called 'Battle of the Sexies'. But now, so as not to offend the 'Woke' and other assorted weirdos, it's become 'Left versus Right'. Won't that offend politicians? But who would care! It's black tie tonight, and being quite high up the loyalty scheme now I have an invite to meet and greet the Captain and his officers. I really don't know if I can be bothered with dressing up! I'll let you know tomorrow.

In the end, I did dress up, and walked into a huge room filled with penguins! I battled to the far end and straight back out, preferring the Crows Nest bar. I was kept out of my room by stewards, as a helicopter was on the way in to pick up another unfortunate soul. So I went and lost a second lot of cash at roulette... but it never was going to be a good night. I miss you.

Alesund today. The sun's shining, and it's quite beautiful. We were here in 2018, in May, and the weather was superb, remember darling? This was the town that burnt down over a hundred years ago; we went on a coach trip, hearing all the history. We visited outlying hamlets, islands, and a church where someone famous is buried. We had a great day. That was a wonderful cruise; on Azura, sister ship to Ventura, with good weather all the way. We did many excursions back then; I really can't face them, now. I'm starting to think that I have a serious problem with depression, but I can't think of an answer.

I'm still searching for the ideal place to write. Today, as most passengers are ashore, I have a table in the window in the main pool area on Deck 9. I'm looking out on Alesund, the hustle and bustle of the port area, and the busy town behind it. Tour boats and small ferries come and go; there's a pint of Italian lager in front of me. I've had worse days. I've decided to rein in my roulette spending, on the theory that if my luck is in, I'll win on the first few spins. It's been three nights now, and my banker number, 29, hasn't come up once! I've not played bingo yet either, I'm really starting to think about money. I wish the damned negligence case could be over, then I might have a chance to plan properly... Whatever that means. I think cruises are off the agenda; there's too much thinking time. I don't want this script to become dark and depressing, but it also has to be an accurate account of my grief trail. In all the wonderful pictures of you in our lounge, you are grinning madly. Even asleep in the sun on Ventura's balcony, you are smiling. The few pictures I have of you after the diagnosis just show a grim, resigned look on your face... I find it hard to look at those last photos. Coppard, bloody cheer up! Many people would give their eye-teeth to be where you are!

We're visiting Olden today dear, the place with your favourite view. The photo is on my sanity wall to prove it. In May 2018, on Azura, we had a table overlooking the rear pool, then on down the valley through snow topped peaks to the glacier. You were mesmerised! With a fizzy water in front of you – of course, I had a Thatchers Gold Cider – that was our best cruise ever. The sun shone from the moment we hit Norway; even in Bergen, notorious for cloud and rain. Do you remember, we were told the teachers always took the kids out on a walk about if the sun showed an appearance! I actually got off the boat today, I booked a ride on the open-topped bus down to the glacier. I thought my bladder could probably cope with that! Supposedly running every fifteen minutes, I sat on it for thirty before it moved off, and it had been there while I was getting changed. So, more like hourly... It was worth it though, the scenery was stunning. Being a Saturday it was very busy, with bikers and campervans galore. We stopped by a tumbling rocky river, the bridge providing a perfect platform for photographs. At the lake at the base of the glacier, a small beach had rocks piled into little pillars, like we used to see by the lighthouse in Lanzarote. I'm sure we did that same trip back in 2018... Oh, if only you were here now, my dearest. Back at the ship, a huge queue waited to board. One gangway was out of action; it took me thirty minutes in the hot sun to get back on. The captain has just announced the departure plan; sixty miles down the fjord to the sea, so three hours of stunning scenery! I'm going back to my balcony to sit for a while with my new camera. I'm not sure anyone will ever see the photos, but any really good ones might make it onto Facebook. Yes dear, I'm on Facebook! Who would have thought?

It's Stavanger today darling, that pretty port where the ship docks right in the town centre, near those picturesque timber houses we wandered around in 2018. We walked to the yacht basin and up to the church overlooking the lake with the swans. We sat and had an ice cream in the sunshine, watching the fountain. It was a bank holiday, so everything was shut, even the cafes – just ice cream and souvenir shops open, which was weird. On the way back to Azura we bought that cute Norway shoulder bag and a little Troll for the summerhouse... you said it looked like me! I just repeated that experience, except I bought a Norway baseball cap this time. I thought I ought to buy something.

It's a sea day tomorrow, and then we'll visit Oslo. I had a bit of a lie in, I'm really enjoying reading again. You know I was always happy to re-read my favourite books. You could never understand that, but then your memory was superb and mine rubbish. I'm revisiting two of Tony's travel books... how he's survived his escapades this long I don't know. I hope he's mellowed now that he's a dad. I went to the 11.15 lecture again today, 'Norway in the Wars.' It was very interesting, and a good time-filler on sea days. The new Lesley Manville film is on today, I was keen to see it as she was at school with me, but the little screening room only holds twenty and has to be booked. It's sold out, bugger! No 'Mrs Harris goes to Paris' for me, then. Instead, I'm sitting in a nice bar on deck 3 above the atrium. It's quite good for writing. I did a bit of laundry in the bath, as the laundrette on sea days is a rugby scrum. I must remember not to get 100% cotton shirts, as they need an iron! Darling, you know my penchant for list making while away... I've been try to budget for the rest of the trip. Sixteen nights is a long time, if I go to the casino every day. Sea days are the longest, so I am going to try just going in the late afternoon. I would like to not go at all, but then I think, why not? If I'm reduced to living on a budget I might get healthier. I need your guiding hand, dear. When we reach Oslo, I'll see where we berth before deciding whether or not to get off for an explore. The weather is still good, but a little cooler at sea. I did two and a half circuits of the promenade deck, nearly a mile – at least I do lots of walking on here! I still feel too misshapen with this damn hernia for the pool or gym, which is a shame because they're nice and quiet. Hm... Perhaps by September.

It's Oslo today, we're moored right in the heart of town opposite the impressive opera house. The city is refreshingly low-rise; tour boats swarm around Arcadia like bees, making us the attraction. A quirky, ramshackle, arts-and-music-centre is just below the rear pool; shipping containers and huge barrels seem to make up the facilities, along with numerous benches. Looks like quite a fun place. Across the water sits a huge lido, bristling with slides and diving boards. It's a Tuesday, but it looks full. Perhaps it's half term here? I had a welcome email from Marianne this morning, she said she wanted to call me today. It seems that after two months, our damned doctors surgery finally passed on my medical records! I could scream. Waiting for the reply as to what time she would call meant I wasn't tempted to go ashore. Besides, from up on deck 10 the far-reaching views are much better than what I'd see at ground level, so I took loads of pictures and called it a day. Marianne called at 1pm. She's going to try to start negotiations, and hopes they don't want an expert witness to look at my notes. I just said do what ever you think best to bring things to a speedy (Hah!) conclusion. Again, I won't hold my breath. I had a salad for lunch, a refreshing change from the roasts; I had ham and a pork pie slice, but it was a pork fillet wrapped in pastry, very nice. What I thought was coleslaw was in fact kimchi; Korean pickled cabbage, which was also surprisingly nice. I'll do a couple of laps of the promenade deck soon, then read until 7.30pm, when I'm having a drink with Tony, a nice old boy I got talking to. I had hoped to avoid roulette tonight, but in truth I'm so bored that I expect I'll succumb. I'm wondering what I'm going to do in September for another sixteen nights... Why did I book it? Actually, this evening was quite lovely; the buffet excelled itself, a Thai green chicken curry and assorted Chinese dishes including delicious spare ribs. I resisted the casino and went looking to have a drink with Tony as usual. There was no sign of him, so I had one drink there, at the Spinnaker bar on deck 2. It was so hot in there that I didn't hang around for a second drink. I sat by the rear pool with a couple of glasses of wine, watching the Oslo Fjord and its islands recede into the sunset. Quite magical, even if the sun never fully set!

It's Gothenburg in Sweden today. Last night the captain mentioned the Volvo museum in his nightly update. I thought, that sounds good, so when I get a signal in the morning I'll see how far away it is on Google Maps. When we docked I was amazed to see it was right beside us on the quayside! Perfect. It's nice here, darling, you would have loved it. We're in the industrial port, but we have Volvo on hand and just behind us is a beautiful inlet with paths and a small marina to amble around. There are a few camper vans parked up behind the ship, looking out over the inlet. They can obviously park there for free! How wonderful. No wonder there are so many camper vans in Scandinavia.

I went around the museum. It was great, with many super exhibits from the early days of motoring right up to modern concept and rally cars. There was even a Saab Viggen fighter jet, I guess Volvo must have worked with Saab on that. I think it was only about £8 for an old boy's ticket, great value. Then I wandered down to the little marina and sat and had a coke. My, I am getting adventurous! Over lunch I thought to myself that I didn't see either of the two Volvos that we had over the years, the 460 or the gorgeous S60, so I went back for a second look. I took the big camera this time. They weren't in there, but I enjoyed it just the same. On the way back, Tony was in his usual bar, so I had a Pellegrino lemonade and chatted to him. It's a sea day tomorrow, so I've decided to do some editing on the book to pass the time.

The sea day was long and tedious, apart from another great lecture on Norway in the war. There was another roast dinner; I'm sick of them now. But I did play roulette twice to pass the time, and was £50 up by the end. I think a cruise any longer than ten days is too much, so note to self: stop booking them, idiot!

GDYNIA POLAND

Oh, what a disappointment! It seems we're berthed in a giant coal bunker within a busy commercial harbour and naval base. The starboard (right) side is berthed next to a coal terminal with ships constantly being loaded and unloaded. There's a smog over the city, and you can taste the coal dust in the air. Not good! The cushions are not being put on the outside seating due to the dust. To port is the naval base, with several small ships in dock. Cargo ferries and container ships constantly pass by. From the top deck I can see that there's nowhere of interest to walk to… It'll be another long day, and we're stuck here till 9.30pm! Damn.

A sea day next, pretty much as usual; the lecture today was at 9.30am, on the Vikings. It was very interesting, especially about building a long ship. I did two laps of the prom, had a pint, then watched Death in Paradise on the tablet. Then lunch, roulette, and a few drinks till cheese and biscuits, and bed. I hope Copenhagen proves to be a good port, with something to walk to.

Hooray! Copenhagen is lovely. There's lots going on in the harbour, and even a sea plane giving tours! We are berthed a ten-minute stroll from the Little Mermaid statue. You would have loved it here, my darling. I had a very pleasant walk to see the statue. There's a small yacht marina on the way, an I even stopped for a beer on the way back – probably the best lager in the world! As with many European cities, there are a lot of canals and all manner of boat trips available. Sadly, I'm too far from Tivoli Gardens, but perhaps a city break some time? No chance! I'm afraid I wouldn't find anything enjoyable without you, my dear, sweet Linda. Those three steps to heaven on the stern railing look more appealing all the time. Yesterday was horrible, I was on my way to write in the afternoon when I passed Tony and his friend in the bar. I said hello, and told him I was going to find somewhere to write. He asked how much was left to do, so I said about 25,000 words. He said, "You best go do it, then." I guess that is the end of that. So I played roulette; £100 gone in 10 minutes, with not one win. I'm only going to play the £125 in chips I have left, so it will be quite a cheap cruise. Afterwards I had two glasses of wine in the piano bar. The second was not my usual brand, 'Holy Snail', a lovely French Sauvignon Blanc, but a horrible stale replacement! They denied it, but I know my wine. I had a last couple out by the pool, the bugger overcharged me by £2 a glass, then asked me if I wanted to meet him by the little mermaid today! Argh, help! I really must stop going on cruises. Iceland will be my last. Only Hamburg left to go now. I really must try and find my park bench, though hopefully not to sleep on this time!

Hamburg... Guess what? We're in the commercial port, so no walk for me today! You recall our very first cruise dear, Hamburg on Cunard's Queen Elizabeth? We loved it, berthed along side the city, with lots to see on the doorstep and of course the water bus for exploring further afield. Twice now with P&O we've docked in this damn wasteland. Only one more sea day, and then home... I can't wait.

Now, the Iceland cruise was always on our wish list. I must do it for the both of us, and I must make it enjoyable. When I get home I'm going to book some excursions, as an incentive to get fit. I'll try to go out later and see some shows and join in the activities a bit more.

It's the last day, so time to pack up. I woke up with a bit of a sore throat and warm ear today... a minor bug, or so I hope. There was another lecture this morning, about the speaker's time in the navy, but what struck me was that over the past attendances there was hardly a cough or splutter. Today there were many coughing fits... I hope it's not Covid on the rise! I shall be glad to get home tomorrow. Walking around the deck just now, I had overpowering memories of holding your hand on our seafront walks. It's strange how things can come back to haunt you – in a nice, but teary way... I miss you, darling. While in this frame of mind, I had a realisation last night, the result of some self analysis. I'm always looking at the negatives, and not realising how lucky I still am. Of course, losing you in that horrible and avoidable way is an absolute tragedy, but it's been over twenty months now and I still haven't pulled myself together. I came to the conclusion that by being so negative, and playing the poor little me card, I was craving the sympathy vote. And then comes the real clincher: just who the hell from? Without you, or even mother to some extent, there is nobody now. All I am doing is slowly alienating the family, friends and neighbours who have stuck by me. It also dawned on me that perhaps I feel guilty for being alive? We often jokingly said we would go together, over a cliff, off the back of a liner, a bottle of pills... but always together. Your damned cancer made that impossible. You, my wonderful girl, wanted me to have a life. And because of you, I have no worries, a nice home, good car and still money in the bank. Although that is depleting quite quickly, mainly because I am a weak-willed idiot. But your memory deserves so much better. I will strive to live up to the legacy you have left me, my wonderful wife. I think that is it for this cruise; many highs and lows, with Gothenburg and Copenhagen being the stars.

43

DAILY LIFE

It's 1st July today. With no trips on the horizon until Iceland on the 29th August, it's a good time to get on with a few routine tasks and get the garden up to scratch. Karen, your WI friend, bought some raspberries and a bit of veg from the allotment round last week. She stayed to look at the garden for a spell, and she was impressed with your roses, my love. My drinking buddy Roy and his partner Kerry are coming next Saturday for hot dogs and a few drinks. I'm very proud of our garden darling, we worked hard to establish it. Their visit will prompt me to do a bit of much-needed housework and garden tidying. I've got a busy week coming up; St Barnabus on Monday, the food bank Tuesday and Wednesday, then I go to your sister's, to put up some more grab handles for Terry. That damned stroke has left him a shadow of his former self. He's very depressed that he can no longer do all the DIY for the family. It reinforces my philosophy of do what you can while you can, and to hell with the cost. Your negligence claim drags on, the opposition now want an expert opinion on both our life expectancies! What a farce. It can only be a guess at best – just another delaying tactic, I suspect. Marianne, our solicitor, is going to try something to force an offer, so fingers crossed.

I had a task pencilled in on the calendar for today; renew my passport! It has six months and one day to run, so with all the horror stories of delays I thought doing it online would be easy. The form is simple enough, but they want a recent photo, even though my Shrek-like features haven't changed since the last one. Now though, it seems the photo booths give you a code and this uploads straight onto the form – no scanning or attachments! I went to Tesco and got all set up, straight faced because smiles are Verbotten! But would the machine take my card payment? No. Credit card? No. The supervisor said the machine's connection had been dodgy for weeks... #@&^!!! To Morrisons next, their machine kept telling me that my pose would not pass the passport test! My head was too low, but there was no seat adjustment... Eventually, after eight attempts, half crouching, I got a pass. £9! Then back on the computer, the form done, and £82.50 paid. Then the last straw: before they action the new passport, they have to have my old passport! WHOA? WHY DID YOU NOT SAY THIS BEFORE! If it's not back by 29th August I'm buggered! What if they don't like my Shrek impression? I dashed to the Post Office and sent it registered post. So now I'll be in a state of panic for weeks... I hate the Civil Service!

But damn, for once they've made me eat my words; I did the online application on Saturday, and the new blue passport popped through the letterbox on Wednesday! Unbelievable. Obviously not all departments are working from home. Or were any humans even involved at all?

44

HAPPY CAMPERS

Apart from a mention of Benny the Bus, and of course Two Clots book earlier, we haven't got into our numerous camping expeditions over the years; the good, the bad and the downright disastrous! We've had tents, four camper vans, a motorhome and two caravans, all with their own tales to tell. Way back in the early days of our marriage, money was tight and camping was a good, cheap option for us. Because you only had an automatic licence we had a metallic green Nissan Sunny 1500 automatic. I loved it; so easy to drive, and quite nippy for the time. One long weekend we took our little two-man tent down to Dymchurch. Somewhere just past Rye, the rear silencer decided to part company from the rest of the exhaust system. Putting it in the boot, and seeing no hope of a 'Gun Gum' bandage patching it up, we carried on, roaring into the campsite early on a Friday evening. We pitched our tent close to a duck pond. The camping field was next-door to a holiday park, with us clearly the poor relations! But it was fun, an adventure. We strolled into Dymchurch along the massive concrete sea wall, and found a little place that did evening meals. I think we had steak, then wandered back, hand in hand, to the sound of waves breaking on the shore.

On Saturday morning we asked in reception for the best town to find a tyre and exhaust centre. Cheriton was suggested; the town where the Channel Tunnel was being built. They were right; our weekend budget took a bit of a hit, but the little Nissan was purring again. We did still splash out on the miniature Hythe-Romney Marsh railway, though. That was a super day out, a museum as well as the ride. We learned that during the war, the train was kitted out with machine guns and patrolled that huge area of coastline. We enjoyed that weekend so much we went back the following spring with your dear mum and dad, staying in a chalet this time. We always wanted to see that area again, but then came your damned illness, bless you.

KAMI THE V W CABRIOLET

Now, Bongle, this is where your infallible memory would be handy! Our adventures with Kami were while we were still at work, so pre-2016, and after we moved to Rustington, so post-2013. It took us about a year to get the place sorted out, so I'd guess it all began in the summer of 2014, and culminated in our grand road trip of June 2015. I'd been toying with the idea of getting a cheap soft-top motor for us to have a bit of fun with. Work had become very tedious for me, scratching around for things to do in my data error correction role to stop me being put on the phone lines and (dread of dreads!) talking to customers! We needed some fun. Already, the idea of early retirement was running through our minds; your sight was decreasing, and our jobs were no longer enjoyable. I considered the options: Mazda MX 5, MG, Triumph Spitfire... nice, but all too low down. The Triumph Stag... Ahh, the dream! But way over budget. Then I started looking at Golf Cabriolets. Affordable, reliable and with a power roof... perfect! I'm not sure you were totally sold on the idea, so while you were on a break with your mum, I went to look at one in Somerset. It was a rural location; I got there about 9 am, and as there was no sign of life, I had a look around it. No effort had been made to prepare it for viewing – it was filthy inside and out, with a split in the roof and poor tyres. I just turned tale and ran for home. I'm not sure I even told you about that disaster! Sorry, darling. But once I had the idea, I couldn't let it go. Browsing eBay, I saw one for £800 cash, at a backstreet car dealer in South London. I made some enquiries. It had a new MOT, was a good runner, and the photos looked good – a dark, metallic blue, although the description said green...? The dealer said that if I got the train up, he would pick me up from the station. I was a bit dubious about carrying all that cash to an unknown place in London, so reluctantly you agreed to come with me. He met us at the station, and took us back to his small showroom. The car sounded good and seemed to drive OK, so it was a bargain. We handed over the cash and got the keys and documents. He even handed us back £20, saying, "You'll need petrol." He was right; as I drove off, the gauge was empty. We made it to a garage two miles down the road. Then the fun started; the electric filler cap release would not unlock. Fumbling in the boot for ten minutes, I was able to release it manually – I suspect that was why he'd never put any petrol in! In the shade of the forecourt I noticed the car was indeed green, but in the sun it had appeared blue. As we drove off I told you about the colour change – that's when we settled on the name, Kami Cabrio, the chameleon! Kami drove sweetly enough; we still had the roof up when we stopped for a late pub lunch in the charming village of Chiddingfold in Surrey. The sun was out, so I said, "Let's put the roof down." Two latches and the press of a button, and the roof rose up above us and folded down above the rear seats. From then on, we both fell in love with Kami. Over the next few weeks I changed the cam belt, front and rear brake pads, and gave her a full service. We visited the big car breakers near Crawley for the fuel cap solenoid, and with a set of alloy wheels and a few bits of trim she was looking good. A new stereo from Amazon saw Kami fit for adventures. At weekends we would go for Kami rides. With the roof down and our favourite CDs blearing out, we were like teenagers. We'd take it to work on nice days and get many compliments. I even made room for her in the garage over winter. I began to have thoughts that we needed to do another Grand Tour to appreciate Kami to the full, so we started to plan. Early June 2015 would be perfect; our anniversary and your birthday, our traditional main holiday time. We booked three weeks each off work, luckily being allowed the same dates.

The Costa Brava in Spain was an area we wanted to explore. So far we'd only spent the odd day or two in the area, on longer forays south. We were in the process of handing back our timeshare; it had changed since it's heyday, but we still had one week in the resort bank to use. Timeshare availability in the Costa Brava is virtually zero, so I booked a mobile home in a holiday park just over the French border for our first week. I'm sure we discussed the arrangements – well, I hope so, but you just left me to get on with it. You know I get as much pleasure from the planning as the actual trip. I really hope I didn't just railroad you into it, but I can no longer check with you to see how you felt. It's nags and doubts like this that are really screwing me up. The main part of the holiday I found on Booking.com, an apartment in the heart of the old town, next to the beach in L'Escala. There was even a covered parking space for Kami. We would start and end the holiday with a bit of luxury, a 48 hour mini-cruise on Brittany ferries to Santander in Northern Spain. Due to the ferry times, we'd have a stay in the local area to get prepared for the adventure; driving through the Pyrenees to cross into France and find our first week's accommodation. Playing it safe and reading the reviews, I'd pre-booked our stopovers for both the outward and homeward journeys. We didn't have sat-nav, so I planned the route at home on Google and printed out pages of place names and road numbers. You hated trying to navigate; your sight was an obvious obstacle, so I tried to make it as easy as possible. And it worked, for the most part!

We got the ferry from Portsmouth, a short hop for us. We had the luxury of a two-berth cabin, with TV and a bathroom; no more reclining seats for us. We had a good meal in the restaurant and a few drinks, of course. The next morning, in the Bay of Biscay, we watched a lecture on the marine life in the area. We spent a couple of hours on deck, supposedly whale watching, not that we spotted anything. By late afternoon on day two, we'd arrived in Cantabria. We drove a few miles to our hotel in Isla, a pretty little seaside resort. We'd been here before on our grand campervan tour in 1994; we had a lovely time wandering around – until you saw a rat on the rocks by the car park! That was enough for you! This time, we were in a lovely little family-run hotel, in a nice room with a sea view. The resort was only really busy in July and August, when the Spaniards from Madrid escaped the heat for their holidays in the north. The beaches were a series of gorgeous sandy coves, very much like Cornwall or Brittany. We had dinner included with our room, local dishes prepared by the owners wife which were really rather good. I think we surprised them when we ordered our second bottle of wine! Next morning, we set off on our adventure. We'd return here for two more nights before our ferry home. Pamplona was our heading for the first stretch towards the Pyrenees; as it was all motorway, we kept the roof up. It's not much fun with it down at 100kmph! Kami was purring along. Not sure what to expect, we told ourselves to fill Kami up every time we got below half a tank. We had a dozen bottles of water as well – better safe than sorry! We were taking a winding course through the mountains and over into France. I'd booked small, rural hotels in picturesque villages. It was quite lovely, just driving for three or four hours before chilling out for the afternoon in a different village each day. In the evenings, we would have the *menu del dia* – usually a tasty regional speciality – and of course, a bottle of the local wine. We also had bottles of red wine to sip on our balconies; the trouble is, they all had corks, and what did your stupid husband forget to pack? We tried all over to get a corkscrew; supermarkets, hardware stores... Eventually, after a couple of days, we came across a barman who spoke good English. He pocketed five euros and gave us one of the corkscrews off the bar! The mountains were as beautiful as we'd hoped, and the roads were well maintained. With the roof down, cruising along, we were having a great time.

We arrived at the caravan park around 1pm on check in day... to bedlam. Absolute chaos! Driving in from the town, we noted that there was no actual path or pavement, a nightmare for you. The milling crowds of youngsters did not bode well for a peaceful week. I found a parking spot and went to find our rep to get the keys. It was best for you to stay in the car; I could tell from your face that you didn't want to be dragged through the cajoling crowds. I found the youngsters who were handling the timeshare caravans. I explained your sight problems and asked if there was a proper path into town. No! So I asked if we were likely to enjoy a peaceful week here... No again! I said thanks but no thanks, they could sleep in our van themselves if they wanted. We were going. You were equally happy to hear that news, so off to Spain we headed. At the border, we stopped for a coffee and to call the agent of our apartment for the second week. "Can we come a week early, and stay for two weeks?" I asked him. No, but he did have a spacious apartment in a small complex in a village on the outskirts of L'Escala. He needed a few hours to get it ready – no problem, as we were still two hours away. Then the heavens opened! We hurriedly got the roof up, but it was hot as Hades inside. If we opened the windows more than a crack, the rain was driven in by the wind. After two hours in the sauna-like car, we got to the agent's home. He was still out, but his wife made us comfortable on their covered terrace, even bringing us a cold drink. The accommodation was quite lovely, nearly new and very spacious. Plus, during the day, while school was in, the pool was empty. We would use the second week in the town centre to stay local; this week we would explore the area. We visited L'Estartit, the Roman ruins at Emporia Brava, Roses, and many other little seaside towns. The village had a bar where we had a beer now and again, but there were not overly friendly. When I asked the barmaid about internet, she just pointed at a sign on the wall with a code... We never did get it to work, we couldn't tell which of the many networks we were supposed to be logging onto. Luckily, the tourist resorts were a lot more welcoming. One morning, at the pool, we got chatting to a nice girl from Wales. She was teaching her toddler to swim. Seems she met a local lad and fell in love; they got married, and moved here. She said it had taken three years for the villagers to accept her, so we had no chance!

We were delighted to move into our apartment in L'Escala. It was on the third floor, with a charming little roof terrace and even an oblique sea view. There was a comfy lounge – the only problem was, it was split level; two steps and no hand rail. You would have to be very conscious of that, my dear. Kami had a nice parking spot in the shade, a double bay built into the basement. The only downside was that the other guests in the larger apartment had a huge Volvo estate. I had to park against the wall, and pull out blocking the road while you scrambled in. Not a real problem, as Kami would only be used for going to the supermarket. We were literally ten seconds from the town beach; crystal clear waters, with a very fine, almost gravel-size shingle. Great! No sand getting into awkward places. The beach was a little cove, with restaurants facing the shore. We soon found a favourite, which also happened to be the closest. We had the same thing virtually every lunchtime: crispy Spanish bacon, two expertly fried eggs, and chips. But the best bit was fresh French-style crispy baguette. We'd make ourselves wonderful sandwiches, dipping them into the eggs. But the swimming was the highlight. The beach was always busy, but not overly crowded during school hours, so ideal for us. There was a small concrete jetty, that strangely did not quite reach the water. We used that as our base; we'd sit on our towels, sometimes with an ice cream, and watch the world go by. The water was wonderfully warm, even for you my darling! We'd splash around, not really swimming – 'Bobbing,' we used to call it. Tiny fish would nibble our toes, which was a bit disconcerting the first few times! There was an off-licence a short walk away; we bought a five-litre flagon of local red wine, then we had it refilled every couple of days at a bargain price. There was a little tourist train; for some reason your family used to call them 'Lolly Trolleys'! We did a circuit on it, leaving the old town and winding around the seafront to the new part of town. Here there were large hotels, a modern promenade, and a bronze statue of a jazz band. My new sun hat blew off, and a young girl picked it up and ran after us to give it back. How sweet! You, of course, were laughing fit to burst! Nearing our starting point, we saw a seafood restaurant, just out of sight of our beach. You would get your beloved seafood after all, dear. We really loved our time in L'Escala. It made a change not to be moving on, or going out in the car every day.

Now it was time to head back to Santander for the ferry. We had the last two nights booked in Isla again for a final relax, so we thought we'd drive a more direct route in the shadow of the Pyrenees, rather than through them. The first day would be a long one, but our reward would be a modern hotel with a superb pool and an elegant restaurant. We set off from our wonderful apartment in L'Escala in beautiful sunshine, with the roof down and wind in our hair. This was to be the day we fell out of love with convertibles; it got hotter and hotter, we were frying. We stopped and put the roof up, but that was worse; without air-conditioning we just could not get it cooler inside. We were dripping, our water bottles were warm… just the thought of that pool kept us going. We pulled into the hotel about 4pm, and after checking in we went straight into the garden to see the pool. Sodding hell! A wedding reception was taking place all around the pool, with the invited brats making full use of the cool water. No way in hell could we waddle through proceedings to have a cooling dip. I went to reception and asked why they didn't warn us; a shrug was the only reply. We dumped the bags and drove off to look for a bar. We weren't going to pay five-star prices for a beer! Just up the road was a great little place – a bar, café, and a base for white-water kayaking. We sat on a long bench overlooking the tumbling river. I went to get two large beers. When I got back, you were overjoyed to find the glasses had been in the freezer! Heaven! That pint didn't touch the sides. We had to have another… It would be rude not to! Back at our hotel, the evening meal wasn't very good. I suspect the head chef had pissed off after the wedding. Ho hum, not what I'd planned. The last day back in Isla did salvage the return journey, though. We had a warm welcome at the family-run hotel, and a nice room with a sea view balcony. Suddenly, the Cantabrian resort had come alive! The short high-season had started; shops and kiosks that were all shuttered up on our outward trip were now doing a roaring trade. We walked on the beach at low tide, between rock formations, flip flops in hand, splashing in the warm waters. Over a beer or three, and an ice cream, we recounted our great adventure. It had been a wonderful trip, and now we had a mini-cruise home to look forward to. We were so lucky to have made so many wonderful memories, my dearest Bongle.

46

THE WAY FORWARD

I had a very bad day last week. It was 4th July. I had the usual Tuesday couple of pints in the Beach Bar with Roy, but on the way home I stopped and bought two bottles of white wine. Lethal. The road was being resurfaced, so I wouldn't be able to use the car for three days; those two bottles were supposed to last till Saturday. As usual, the TV was dire. I flicked around, all the time drinking... Yes darling, the two bottles went. Bugger. The next morning, I thought I was dying. I had a blinding headache, stomach cramps, and a mouth like a cess pit. I didn't touch a drop more booze for three days, and then only in sensible proportions. I think I may have come to a turning point; I have finally got it through my thick head that you are gone, my gorgeous lady, and revelling in self-pity is helping nobody. It may even be alienating some people. You wanted me to have a life. It may not be the life I want, but something must be better than this. So, white wine, my nemesis, is out of the window. I just want to be a social drinker, like normal people. I spend a small fortune on trips and cruises, but haven't been taking advantage of the scenery or activities and shows... that's just stupid.

I mean, look where I am now, writing in the Beach bar, being waited on by the best staff a joint could have. The sun's out, but the wind is blowing a gale – the kite surfers are loving it! There's a pint of cider in front of me, dogs bounding through the surf... It's gorgeous, and I can do this every day! Why the bloody hell should anyone feel sorry for me?

So, in keeping with my new philosophy, I've set plans in motion for the rest of the year. To hell with money – I have to forget about the negligence case, it's doing my head in. I go to Iceland on the 29th August, and I've booked a sun cruise for just before Christmas. No kids, same old places, but this time I will get off for a wander. I'm in the process of booking a road trip to Snowdonia, one of our most beloved places, and via Ironbridge, another spot from our wish list. I am so lucky – thank you, darling – to have this beautiful Honda driving machine, and it needs using. I saw a show: Greg Wallace, A Weekend in York. That's another place that was always on our to do list... Perhaps I'll do it by train – if the buggers ever stop striking! Nothing changes, darling.

We live in such a wonderful place. The people in our little close are quite lovely! A new couple, Jo and Tony, live opposite now, on the ground floor. Jo asked me for a lift to the doctor's today. She has COPD like me. I was happy to oblige, and have chance to chat.

Poor Patricia had her garden wall knocked down, again – the *sixth* time! It was Amazon's fault this time. Quite a little community we moved into, and we became a part of it, my darling.

I've mentioned how, in an effort to ensure all our wonderful holiday photos were safe, I copied all our pictures that were on CDs onto a hard drive. Remember, we sat and watched them all one winter's afternoon before you were diagnosed?

It was wonderful, recapturing our many adventures, rather like this book. Now I transferred all your medical files and spreadsheets onto the drive, so I didn't have constant reminders of your illness on the computer. Since then, that hard drive has refused to open, or even be recognised by the TV or computer. Part of me thinks, well who is ever likely to see them again? Then I thought, I want to. I found a local computer specialist in Wick, just along the road. They've managed to capture the data and I'm waiting for Amazon to deliver another hard drive. A different brand, I might add! Then they'll transfer the files, for the princely sum of £150! Ouch. I might have to celebrate by getting some new additions to the photo wall. Also, sometimes it's nice to share a memory on Facebook. I can't believe how much I use social media now, Bongle! But then I used to have you, and that was all I ever needed. I got the new hard drive, and have now uploaded the files of pictures, from 2002 through to the Arctic cruise in 2020. That was our last real holiday, darling. I intend to go through them, delete the poor ones, and save them back onto the hard drive for safe keeping.

Roy, my Tuesday drinking buddy, and his partner Kerry, are on an Artic cruise next March. They've been quizzing me about our experiences, so I decided to put all our Norway photos from both the winter and summer cruises on a USB stick for them. I have to tell you, my darling, just looking at those two sets of pictures had me in tears and I fairly cracked up. It may take me some time to review all the images and all the wonderful memories and experiences they contain.

47

EAST SUSSEX: DOWN MEMORY LANE

It's 21st July, and I thought a little break might be in order. I wanted a nice driving road to get some fun out of Evie (the CRV Hybrid). The roads around Beachy Head fitted the bill, with a night away and a visit to Sheffield Park in the morning. I set off on the A27 and dropped down to Newhaven. From there I drove to Pevensey Bay, where we had many adventures over the years. On the outskirts of Seaford I turned right towards the seafront, past the Buckle campsite. We had one of our first adventures there, darling, when we were young, fit and adventurous. That would have been in Pooh the Bus, the VW we took on our grand tour of Europe in 1994. I pulled into the car park where we went with the mums once; they chatted and looked at the sea view while we went for a walk. I recall they said not to rush back! The cheek.

On leaving Seaford, I switched Evie into sports mode and followed the twisting A259 down by Cuckmere Haven. Up the steep, sheep-covered hill, and right at East Dean, past the wonderful Tiger Inn to Birling Gap – a super fun drive. The National Trust card finally got some use to pay for the car park. Birling Gap is now looked after by the trust; it has a big car park, a toilet block, and a nice shop and café. It was much the same as our last visit, but the views along the coast to the Seven Sisters cliffs are the main attraction. Such a superb vista! They've built a viewing platform and a zigzag steel staircase down to the beach. The platform is in great demand by visitors, all vying for position to get the best vantage point for photos. I even got my trekking poles out and climbed the hill behind the coastguard cottages to get a better picture. Yes, the new camera is getting an outing, too! There are only three cottages left now, the rest of the terrace having crumbled into the sea, but still some idiots go right up to the cliff edge. All the time on this drive, images flood into my head. We've toured this area in cars, camper vans, caravans and the motorhome. Now though, it's just me. It's not the same, but I am savouring our memories, my dear. I had a Sicilian lemonade – being good darling, but it was only 11am – and a Cornish pasty, that was dry and peppery as I knew it would be. I cruised by Beachy Head, just stopping to get a photo of Eastbourne Bay. There's a Ferris wheel at the west end of the beach now. It seems like a bit of a waste, as the best view of all from the cliff-tops is just up the road. Then I drove to the Sovereign shopping centre, as we used to when camping in Pevensey Bay. This also reminded me of my dear cousin Jane, languishing in a nearby Hospice. She was so young and in such torment. We used to take her for days out, and sometimes to our flat in Hove. She used to beg us to let her stay, but we couldn't look after her there. Never did we dream then that a similar tragedy would engulf us. In Asda I got a nice pair of slip-on casual shoes and two packs of pants. You would have chucked most of mine out ages ago! I walked to that pub on the first floor, in the marina we used to visit. It seemed a bit weird being there without you, Bongle, but then everything does now. I filled up with petrol at Asda – damn,

5p cheaper here than we have to pay! I wanted to cruise back to Birling Gap to use the loo before going up the Jevington road by East Dean. So many of our early adventures in the camper happened at Filching Manor, with the superb motor museum. We even got shown around by the charming resident lord of the manor; Halbard, I think the name was. I recall we even took my mum and Ruby dog there for a day out in the van once. Ruby got us in trouble for snuffling someone's picnic! She was a minx where food was concerned. It's so strange how memories like that flood back, but I cannot remember yesterday's dinner! I passed the Eight Bells pub at Jevington; we walked there one lunchtime from the manor. It was a darned sight further than we'd thought, and there were no pavements, but I do recall a wonderful pie! I'm staying in Halland, on the A22 tonight. It's a funny old place called Buffalo Bill's – a motel and Tex-Mex restaurant. It's all a bit tired, but friendly, though. I keep expecting TVs Alex Polizzi, The Hotel Inspector, to show up. Still, it fits the bill tonight. It's a short run to Sheffield Park tomorrow, although the weather forecast isn't good. I think I'll try the ribs tonight. I don't think I can manage an 8oz burger anymore!

The motel is just up the road from the Marquis dealership at Golden Cross, where we bought our last caravan. And, coincidently, where we bought all the conversion parts for our wonderful Benny the Bus. Oh darling, we did so much, but should have had a few more years before us! I get so angry. Why you? With all those horrible people that keep surviving... I know, calm down dear... but that phrase never worked, did it? So, back to Marquis. Seeing all the motorhomes parked along the Beachy Head roads made me wonder yet again, would it suit me now? Or would it just be another waste of time and money? With hotels there is all the packing etc, which is a pain. A small motor home would be a home from home. They do some lovely sub-six-metre ones now, and automatic. Also there are some lovely micro caravans now – that would leave my lovely car available for days out, whilst still being the everyday drive. But it's all pie in the sky until your negligence case is resolved. If ever!

Right, a shower now, and dinner. I'll let you know how it goes, and if the weather lets me get to Sheffield Park. Goodnight my dear, I love you.

Well, dinner was a surprise! I went for a 'Cowboy combo', cringe cringe… a 6oz steak and a half rack of ribs, with corn cob, slaw and curly fries. The steak was ok, but the ribs were the best I've ever had, so much meat on them and very tender. I was very impressed! The bed was comfy enough, but I decided to head for home at 7am, as the forecast said it would be pouring down by the time Sheffield Park opened. All in all, I enjoyed the drive, but I don't really think road trips and hotels are my answer. But then is anything?

I bought a copy of MMM, the motorhome magazine at the weekend. I like to keep abreast of the news; there were several readers' letters bemoaning the rocketing site fees of the two main clubs, and having to book and pay a deposit. I think if I did go back to it I'd find it a shock how thing have changed since lockdown. I'm in the doldrums again, wondering what to do for this school holiday period. The kitchen tap has been weeping from the base for a while; I had a replacement that I bought when Lidl did an offer, so I changed it today. My god Linda, I'm not the man I was. A few short years ago it would have been a breeze. My mobility has declined by a scary degree – after ten minutes on my knees, they were in agony. I had planned to clean behind all the appliances, and in the sink cupboards as well, but I got the tap changed and called it a day. I keep saying it: I have to loose weight and get fitter. But

I'm devoid of willpower. I always was, till you came along and gave me a reason and a purpose. I really do worry for my future now. I know that giving up drinking is the key, but it's my only real way of socialising. I know, that sounds pathetic. I'm slowly looking at all our photos again... pleasure and pain in equal measure. I'm up to Bavaria and Austria in 2005. I put four of them on Facebook as a memory, and people love them! We had such a great time; not a care in the world back then, and smiles all the way. I suppose, compared to many folk we can't complain, but it still seems so unfair, especially after all the hip and eye issues that dogged your life. I suppose that's what made you enjoy everything to the full, with a grin from ear to ear. I get a lot of comfort from your perpetual smile, darling. I've just had a pep-talk from Sue, one of the lovely ladies working at the Beach Bar. I showed her the Facebook pictures, and I mentioned what an ordeal today's bit of DIY became. I said I was thinking of trying the gym again, but she debunked that, saying I'd be better walking and using my bike regularly. She even suggested riding around our numerous private estates for a bit of variety, as she did during Covid. She's right; there are so many machines in the gym that my damn hernia would stop me from using, so walking and cycling are the obvious choices. Now I'm in a quandary as to which of our many adventures to write about next. I think I'll browse through our recovered photographs and see what leaps out at me. Yesterday I visited Jane and Terry at their home, adjoining the lovely place Laura and her husband Lee bought in Small Dole. They were preparing their new motorhome for a trip to France. It was nice to catch up with them, so the logical choice for the next travelogue has to be Brian!

OUR ADVENTURES WITH BRIAN THE MOTORHOME

Brian, as all people of our age will know, was the snail from BBC's Magic Roundabout. He carried his home on his back – and so did we, for some very enjoyable adventures. You recall my dearest, that when we decided to leave EDF Energy in 2016 (and I thank heavens we did), a motorhome was very much on our minds. The VW Campers were great fun when we were younger and fitter, but now we needed a bit of comfort. Some luxury even, and most definitely an on board shower and toilet! Oh Bongle, we had some fantastic trips in camper vans in our first ten years of married life. France, Spain, Portugal... but in retirement we were looking to explore our own British Isles a lot more, particularly Scotland and Wales. You, my dear, also had a hankering for the Emerald Isle, though sadly we never got that far. I'd been reading motor home magazines for years, keeping abreast of models and technical queries. As an ex-mechanic, I found them very interesting. Our parking space in front of the garage would easily accommodate a six-metre van. I removed some turf alongside the concrete and laid plastic grids that grass would grow back through, so we could have our car along side. We'd spent the last three years getting the flat and garden up to scratch and now it was time for us to have some 'me' time! With a van I would have endless 'pottering' to keep me happy, and you had just started to enjoy crafting and painting and of course your beloved talking books. We wouldn't be bored!

But which van? We went to our local dealer, a few miles up the A24, and looked at a few. You were taken by a model with a nice interior and a mid-lounge; two small settees behind the front seats that made up into a double bed. It was in nice condition. But I knew making up that bed every night would get to be a pain, and the Fiat base vehicle was the old, pre-2007 version, which is what I was thinking of to keep up residual values. There are literally hundreds of makes and models to choose from, and the internet is great for research, but until you get inside it you can't be sure. We were talking about 20K plus here, a huge outlay for us back then. Looking on Google maps, there was a trio of large dealerships within a few miles of Poole, so a weekend away was on the cards. The central Travelodge was booked, and off we went! We were a bit overwhelmed by all the different makes and layouts that were on offer, but then we saw Brian. A two-berth, coach-built motorhome converted by Swift, a trusted brand; Sundance 590 PR was the model. It looked huge, but was only 6.3 metres long. An electric double step made entry to the side door easy. Inside we immediately fell in love. The comfy front captain's seats gave a commanding view of the road; collapsible blinds would seal the cab area at night. Behind the drivers seat was the washroom, shower, basin and electric flush loo – that made me happy. Backing onto the washroom was a large fridge, with gas, electric or 12 volt options, plus a wardrobe and a gas fire. The TV bracket was on the back wall of the wardrobe. On the opposite side, behind the door, was the work top – a four-burner hob, one being electric, a sink and drainer as well as an oven and grill. But it was the rear lounge that sold it to us. U-shaped, with two side settees six-foot three-inches long, that we would use as our oh so easy single beds. Roof vents were above the lounge and another near the front. It was perfect! On board fresh and waste water tanks, blown gas hot air heating, plus the fire, and hot water. You, my dearest, really liked the idea of not having to brave the campsite shower blocks. It was not a problem if they had disabled facilities where we could go together, but the single sex ones were hell for you, not being able to see much. We went for a test drive, and in a few minutes I was at ease. After all, it was smaller that the Ford Cargo truck I had driven for Parcel Force, even if that was fifteen years earlier! You, Bongle, were impressed with the comfort and the high position. You loved being able to see over fences and hedges. £22500… Ouch! But Brian was perfect for us. We had grand plans for many years of touring, both at home and in Europe. We paid a deposit on the understanding that I just had to measure our parking to ensure that 6.36 metres of van would fit. It would… just!

We were excited, but a little miffed to learn that it would be a month before we could pick Brian up, due to summer season demands on the workshop. But as they would do a full service and habitation check, we had to wait.

When the day finally came, we were like children on Christmas morning. We got the train to Poole and one of the staff picked us up. At the showroom, Brian was parked next to the office, connected to the mains electricity. We had a bewildering hour's handover, being told all about Brian's technical bits and bobs – heating, water, toilet and a myriad of other technicalities. You just said, "That's your department, dear!"

We drove off in a state of ecstasy. There was a huge Asda superstore close to the dealer, so we parked up at the far side of the car park where Brian had loads of space. We went on a spending spree, buying melamine crockery, plastic glasses, cutlery, sheets, quilts, all manner of equipment we would need. Driving home, we were tempted to stop off in the New Forest for a trial run... But alas, we knew we were not yet fully equipped for a stopover.

When Brian was safely parked on the far side of the drive, his nose just level with the pavement and his rear just six inches from the garage, I realised it would be a good idea to sink a kerbstone into the surface. This would act as a backstop for Brian's rear wheels, to prevent an accident with the garage. So the job list began... and not just the jobs. The amount of equipment and accessories we still required was amazing, and not exactly cheap, but once acquired it would provide us with years of economical adventures.

And so the Amazon orders started; electric hook up cable, water hose (food grade), connectors, chemicals, cleaners... we were horrified how it was all adding up. But Brian was to be our retirement dream, and would be with us for years. Oh darling, if only. We needed a television, but one that worked on 12 volts as well as mains, and a compact CD player for those winter evenings. A good sat nav was also on the list; a special one for motorhome owners, that we could program Brian's dimensions into and it would steer you clear of low bridges and single tracks roads. Of course, the damn thing didn't actually do that – we got caught out a few times! One of the first things a new owner should do is print off a crib card, with length, width and most important height, in metric and imperial values, and stick it to the sun visor so it's instantly available. We were nearly ready to roll, but reversing was a bit of a problem. Now vans have cameras, but we didn't. I know you would be panicked if I asked you to spot me into a gap or a parking space... I definitely can't blame you, it was amazing how you did what you did with that little bit of sight. I watched a YouTube video on installing reversing beepers; it looked pretty straight forward, so I ordered a set, in grey to match the bumper. And a hole cutter... gulp! Cutting six holes in our bumper did fill me with dread, but those seven short years ago I was a lot fitter and more dexterous. I also invested in quality tyre inflator that could cope with the 70 psi van tyre pressures, and a three-ton trolley jack, as I'd be maintaining Brian myself. Over time, we would do countless little modifications; little things to make life easier, like you sewed hanging tapes onto all our van towels and tea cloths. Simple, but so handy.

We started to load the van, so that it would be ready to go at a moment's notice. We had van sauces and condiments, tea, coffee, hot chocolate, toiletries and personal gear. We had two spacious overhead lockers each above the lounge, with the large rear one reserved for bedding. The huge space under the bed was for outdoor leisure gear and shoes, and we shared the wardrobe. At last we were ready – but where to go? We wanted a fairly close site just for a few nights. We'd joined both the big clubs, Camping and Caravanning and the Motorhome and Caravan club... the total outlay of this venture is not for the faint hearted!

49

NEWSFLASH

Marianne your case solicitor rang yesterday. The medical expert has concluded his work to determine our life expectancy. It was horrible to hear that you should have made 79 – thirteen extra years, had you had the correct treatment. Oh god, my poor darling. I was not surprised at all to learn that I can expect just another eight years, if I carry on with this life of self destruction. I'm not too upset at eight years, I'm not exactly enjoying life without you, Bongle. But that time must be healthy years. I am in the Beach Bar enjoying my last two pints of cider. The lovely Kat is leaving today; she's been a good friend these past two years. So, my new regime starts tomorrow. But I did get up at 6am this morning, poured the rest of the wine down the sink, and went for a bike ride to your memorial bench slat. If there is a plus side to this, it's that the case can move into the final stages of settlement. About bloody time! Although the figure asked for will be a bit reduced, which I find ironic as by letting you die they are in effect killing me. This has to end soon so I can move on... The weather for the weekend is rubbish, which will not help my will power. Still, there's lots of housework, so I'll try to keep busy.

50

BACK TO BRIAN, OUR HAPPY THOUGHT

The club site to the east of Chichester on the A259 was our chosen trial campsite. Not too far, with a bus stop right outside the next-door pub, and ideal for visiting Havant and Hayling Island. Perfect! It was a relatively small site, but with a superb disabled washroom; we'd come here many times for an impromptu break.

We arrived and checked in, asking for an accessible pitch not too far from the facilities. First we stopped at the water point to fill Brian's on board water tank. We had a separate five-litre bottle for hot drinks, and bottled water for drinking. We didn't know how sterile the on board tank was; that job was on the to do list.

First we set up camp; electrics on, fridge switched over, TV aerial aligned, and awning out with chairs and picnic table set up. Then it seemed a good idea to check out the next-door pub. We had a nice couple of drinks on the front terrace, feeling pretty contented with ourselves. We would dine alfresco tonight, outside the van; we had wine in the fridge and a pasta bake and salad to go with it. We were, to use your phrase darling, made up. We slept very well, the breeze rusting the trees, moonlight streaming in through the skylight... we loved it. After breakfast, the chores had to be done. You did the washing up in the van, while I sorted out the rubbish and emptied the toilet cassette. Today we would catch the bus to Havant, and another on to Hayling Island. We loved it, bumbling around on the seafront. A little train ran along the length of the beach to the pleasure park. We had a snacky brunch in a cafe, then a couple of beers in the seafront pub. It was great not to be driving for a change! We spent another cosy evening in the van. Rain had come in the late afternoon, so we ate indoors. We couldn't believe how comfortable we were! At night, the rain pattering on the roof was very calming... Oh darling, we'd definitely done the right thing in buying Brian. As it was late summer, we'd have a few more short breaks, but for now it was all about planning our longed-for tour of Scotland's famous five-hundred-mile coastal route. We aimed for next April, before it got too busy and before the dreaded midges came out to torment folk.

For short-range adventures we were lucky, with Chichester to the west, then the New Forest a bit further on. With wonderful Dorset also within two hours, we were spoilt for choice. To the east there was one of our favourites, a club site near Battle. It had lovely grounds, with Bexhill and Hastings to the south and many National Trust sites in easy reach. There was also the site by the beach in Pevensey Bay... Oh darling, writing all this is really making me want to get another van. It would not be the same without you, but it would give me an active hobby and be a great writing base. But there is absolutely nobody to talk this over with who would have any understanding whatsoever.

51

SCOTLAND OR BUST!

It was a trip long in the planning. Brian was loaded with every conceivable thing we might need, when we set off one April morning for the Highlands. There was no rush; we'd have two overnight stops on our way to the border, the first being in the Midlands, in the grounds of an adventure park, and the second around Carlisle. You placed 'Monk Monk' – a little furry toy monkey I bought you one Valentines day – on the dashboard, propped up to enjoy the view. We were a bit soft about naming things, silly old sods. The first night we ate out, as the adventure park had a selection of restaurants and also some nice gardens to walk around. That was a relief, after sitting in the van all day. Our second long driving day was uneventful, except our campsite was a bit hard to find, being close to our route, but rural. It was a basic site, with no toilet block but set in wonderful garden grounds. Brian proved his worth by having everything we needed for a comfortable stay; hot food and chilled wine... We were loving the adventure!

The next day we crossed the border near Gretna Green. Very romantic, not that we saw much of it from the highway. The infamous town of Lockerbie was our first stop, having a large Co-Op with a fuel station. Stocked up and fully-fuelled, we had next to get through Glasgow en route to Luss, on Loch Lomond. Glasgow traffic was not as bad as I feared and once past it the road turned into a pleasant route. Loch Lomond is surprisingly close to Glasgow, but it's like a different world. We had tantalising glimpses of the waters as we headed ever northwards. Our club site was right on the water's edge; two separate areas, each with its own toilet/shower block and facilities. On check in, one of the lady wardens said, "Follow me on my bike and I'll take you to your pitch." We followed her to the far area, where she directed us to a gravel hard standing pitch with electric hook-up. I asked if it was OK to drive on forwards, so our lounge would face the Loch for our two nights here. "Fine," she said. The view was glorious! A shame it was grey skies, but then it is Scotland. We set up camp in the now well-rehearsed routine. You had your tasks, Bongle, and I had mine; we made quite a team. There was a couple in a newish VW camper two pitches away from us, and the only others were a family of five in a tent fifty yards away on the grass. There were even washing machines and tumble dryers available, not that we needed them yet. But we would – we hoped to be away about a month if all went well. We wandered along the shoreline to the village of Luss, to a little jetty used for lake tours in the high season. It was a great vantage point for photos. The village shop was very touristy; we bought some postcards to send to the folks, and some very pretty highland wildlife stamps. A shame the small print said you couldn't actually use them! We had a drink in the hotel bar, common up here instead of pubs. It was all old stone, with a huge fireplace, but the menu prices reflected the fact we were in a tourist hot spot. Good job Brain was waiting to feed us when we got back! We'd packed our small slow cooker; right now a pot of homemade chilli was bubbling away. With rice, tortilla chips, grated cheese and sour cream, it would be superb – not to mention the wine, of course. As we wandered back, the sky was darkening and we felt the first spots of rain. Back in Brian, I struck up the gas fire to take the chill off, while you readied the plates. There was a CD and radio in the cab with extra speakers in the lounge, so we could have music or TV; Brian really was a home from home. As we sat in our super-cosy lounge, we felt a twinge of sympathy for the couple in the little VW, and downright horror at the plight of the family in the tent, as the rain started to hammer down! We fell asleep to the beat of rain on the roof, and it was still pouring as light crept into to lounge. Well, the bedroom, at this moment in time. It was surprising how comfortable those side sofas were as single beds. The morning routine started, usually by me getting up to pop the gas fire on, and if particularly chilly, as it was that morning, the blown hot air heating as well. The hot air was your favourite in the early mornings. An outlet was at the bottom of your sofa/bed base, and you would slide your quilt over until the warm air was ducted right under your quilt! It's remembering little things like that that set me off again. Of course, while I was up I made the tea, and put it on the cabinet in between our beds. As a holiday treat we had two each of your favourite Moo Cow biscuits... You and your funny names! Malted Milk, with a cow on them, hence Moo Cow biscuits! While savouring the tea and biccies, I began to wonder if we could fit the family in the tent in here for a hot drink and a warm up, perhaps even some toast. But when I looked out of the front cab window, I saw they were in the last throws of breaking camp. I hoped they'd enjoyed some of their time here. We felt like royalty, comfy as we were in Brian; no cramped confines for us. After a second cup of tea and an hour's reading, the rain stopped and the sun broke through. As we'd almost certainly have the shower block to ourselves, we'd use those facilities today. It was lovely and warm in the disabled shower room, with loads of space and hanging hooks for a change. Luck was with us, and the day stayed warm and dry. We only had another twenty-four hours here, so it was silly to drive anywhere. We'd explore locally – which meant Luss again, but a bit more leisurely this time. We ambled back to the jetty by the main car park, disappointed that the Loch boat trips wouldn't start for a few more weeks. The car park was filling up with coaches, as this was one of the few places on the Loch that could cater for them. The village must have been a very different place before tourism. The stone cottages would have had some form of work being done inside, weaving or spinning no doubt. I suspect current property prices would be well out of our league, darling! We had a pleasant, if a tad expensive, lunch in the hotel bar. The fire was lit today, I expect because of the earlier downpour. Wandering back to Brian, we chatted and agreed that less touristy spots probably suited us better, beautiful as Loch Lomond was. So next morning we were eager to get on the move, into the real Highlands. Glencoe was our next booked campsite, and we even knew the wardens there, as we'd met them at a club site in Crowborough, just before they were due to move up here. The journey was superb, even though the road was winding and rather narrow. We rose up through the pine-clad hills, stopping for a mid-morning coffee. Oh, the joy of motor-homing, and being self contained, was wonderful.

We climbed the steep road approaching that famous valley. As we crested the brow, Glencoe was laid out before us, winding down to the distant shore of Loch Leven. There was a small gravel car park off to the right, perfect for taking in the vista at leisure. I reversed Brian in and we moved into the lounge to take in the view, as the clouds scudded across the sky. Intermittent sunshine created shadows, and changed the colours of the rocks and mountain slopes. I put the kettle on, and some bacon on the grill for a sandwich, while you slowly scanned in the scenery, mesmerised. We continued down the valley and somehow managed to miss the turn off to our club site, which was on the outskirts of the village. Unfortunately, this allowed us to see the commercial campsites right down on the loch shore, in the heart of the community. I was sure I'd made a mistake booking the club site. Of course, you said nothing, but I do wonder if you didn't think, 'idiot!' to yourself.

We booked in and set up camp, after which we had a little explore. The road to the village and Loch Leven didn't even boast a foot path, a nightmare for us with me having to guide you. I'd planned to use this site as our base for the area, and our steam train ride from Fort William in a couple of days. As it was, we'd have to pack the van and drive just to have a beer! Idiot. I went to see our friendly wardens, and explained that as you, my dear, were registered blind, we couldn't even walk to the village from there. Could we please leave tomorrow and get a refund for the other booked nights? With some excitement, we broke camp the next morning. I'd managed to get us a pitch on a site called Bunroy. It was a few miles past Fort William, down the road leading to Ben Nevis. Right by a river, with a restaurant and bar opposite the camp entrance... perfect! We were very happy there. We could walk by the river, go for a drink and a meal, everything we needed was just a stroll away. Next day we would go to Fort William to stock up on supplies, and to check out the parking for Brian. The following day we were booked on The Hogwarts Express to Mallaig via the Glenfinnan viaduct. We needn't have worried; a large Morrisons supermarket adjoined the station, which also had a large car park with some bigger bays for motorhomes. We could see the steam train puffing away in the station, getting ready to depart. The sound was magical, quite apt for the Hogwarts Express! When we got back to the site and set up camp again, the routine was already becoming ingrained for us. Looking at caravans on adjacent pitches, we could see the attraction of having a car for days out, but I didn't really like the idea of towing. Of course, my dearest, before your sight worsened we would have had bikes with us. The convenience of Brian was winning for now; the ability to just pull into a lay-by and pop the kettle on and knock up a snack was a definite benefit. That evening we wandered over to the bar for a couple of pints. Cider for me and lager, in halves of course, for you, Bongle. Back in Brian we settled down for a chicken and bacon pasta bake with garlic bread – and, of course, a bottle of white wine.

Monday dawned; the day of our train ride! I'd waited to book the Monday, figuring the weekend would be packed. With Brain safely parked up (for an exorbitant fee, as Morrisons had a two hour time limit), we entered the station. It was very busy. I was glad we didn't have to queue for tickets. On the platform, the engine was steaming away, surrounded by people desperate to get a good photo. A few folk were dressed as pupils of Hogwarts; of course, kiosks were flogging expensive memorabilia, including Berty Botts' all flavour beans. In reality these were just jellybeans that should cost a few pence. We were crammed into a compartment with four other eager travellers, including two from America. The journey was quite scenic, lots of bays and sandy coves, the Glenfinnan Viaduct... Well, you didn't actually see much of it from the train. On the ground though, many people were getting wonderful photos of the steaming engine high above!

We should really have driven the scenic road in Brian and parked below to get the best view. In Mallaig, a pretty little harbour town where a ferry runs over to Skye, we were astounded to find virtually everything was shut! Most of the restaurants and even the fish and chip shop closed on a Monday – for a tourist town, this was terrible. We squeezed into a pub; there were no tables to be had, but we did get a pint. Then we returned to the station and had a pasty in the café there. All in all, a bloody expensive mistake. We could have driven the road, had super views, and a great lunch in Brian, all for free! Idiot. Again! But tomorrow we would head north, into the wilds of Skye… Oh please, let it be good.

The drive through the Highlands was quite wonderful. Do you remember Lin, we came across a Bronze memorial statue of three Royal Marine Commandos? We pulled in to stretch our legs. I said a few words about my wonderful uncle Arthur, who was in that regiment and took part in the Normandy landings. Quite a thoughtful interlude. We pressed on and drove by the Loch. In the distance, the Skye bridge became visible, so we pulled into a lay by on the approach to get a photo of this iconic structure. We were very excited. You were desperate to see Highland cows, along with stunning scenery. Our campsite was very rural, on the shores of Kinloch, not far from the Dunvegan estate. We needed a supermarket to stock up for a few days; Portree was the main town, and had a fair sized Co-Op. We took the opportunity to fill Brian's tank as well. The campsite was superb, with modern facilities – even a drive-over waste water drain point – and Highland cows were in the field next door! Wow. We had a hard standing pitch with electricity, and a drain so that our waste water could go straight out. I reversed in, so our lounge faced the loch, with a view of the cattle to the side. The wonderful wardens also owned the farm, so tasty fresh eggs were on sale in the site shop along with a few other treats, like homemade bread. We walked over for a closer look at the magnificent cattle. The farmer/warden was by the fence, and he told us that in the summer months he couldn't house the cows in the main field alongside the road, as tourists would block the road to get photographs! We campsite residents had the cattle all to ourselves, and I think everyone took a copious amount of pictures. Of course, exploring entailed packing up Brian and getting mobile, so we only ventured out for two of the five days. The first, to the must-see Old Man of Storr just North of Portree, was a scenic drive by sea and lochs. The approach was packed with cars, so we found a car park with a good distant view and settled for that. We never would have made the climb on the scree covered slope anyway, never mind climbing the rock. We stayed in camp the next day for a bit of housework and laundry. At home these would be chores, but in Brian it was all part of the adventure. Our final foray was a little drive along the Loch to the Dunvegan estate, a big country house with gardens. It was private, but open to the public – trouble is, the prices were astronomical! So we decided to wait for the National Trust; our next site had one just down the road. We were sad to leave such a well-equipped and run campsite, but unless you were into hiking we had pretty much 'done' Skye. Our next stop was Inverewe. On Google it looked like it could be the highpoint of the trip – literally, as we intended to head south again before the peak season began. Now, when telling people about this trip, many warned us of the awful midge misery. My research showed that Avon's 'Oh So Soft Moisturiser' was an excellent deterrent, even used by the forces. So I ordered six bottles... and we never saw a single midge or used a drop! Early season, I guess.

Heading north again, it was a scenic pretty drive. We could see why this costal route was so popular. The road was two lanes, but I could imagine in peak season with large motorhomes and caravans on the move, it could become a nightmare. We would pass Applecross, a coastal village with a superb campsite. I'd looked at it, but the access route was notoriously difficult for large vehicles. Darling, you would have been terrified if you needed to be lookout on blind bends, so we stuck safely to the main A-road. We passed glorious little granite fishing ports and white sandy coves... even the weather was behaving itself. We swept down a glen beside a rocky, fast-flowing river. As we approached Inverewe, we came to a T-junction. The Loch was before us, the hotel and restaurant to the left, and the campsite sign pointed right, so right it was. A few yards further along was the village hall, with a very welcoming campsite beside it. The front row of pitches were by the road directly looking out on the Loch – wonderful! We were enchanted and very happy. When we checked in, all the front row spots were taken, mainly by long term caravanners. Still, we had a pitch one row back, slightly elevated so we had a good view of the steely water. The usual setting up camp routine was followed, with a cup of tea and biscuits midway. Hand-in-hand, as always, we explored. First we crossed the road to sit on a bench and take in the view. We were at the end of a long finger of water; to the left a craggy coastline extended down to the sea. Later, we'd explore wartime fortifications on that side. To the right was a gentler landscape, a large house with what looked like exotic trees reaching down to the shore. That must be the National Trust property! And within walking distance, too. The shower block was clean, but there was no disabled shower, so you'd get to wash in Brian. That didn't bother you at all. The site shop stocked the basics, but the village store was pretty good, down by the hotel. The only downsides were that the TV signal was not great (we had DVDs to compensate) and the site WiFi was rubbish. To use the internet at all required standing right outside reception... But that wasn't a big deal back then. The site noticeboard proclaimed a craft fair in the village hall on Saturday, which was tomorrow. That first evening we wandered along to the hotel bar. Being a Friday, it was packed. Doing my usual thing (which you hated!), I said to the barman, "Take one for yourself." He said, "and my colleague?" I said yes... Idiot! It turned out there were four frigging colleagues, not much change from my twenty! I was just taken as another mug tourist. Having been in the hospitality game many times over the years, it was common courtesy to offer staff and fellow managers/licensees a drink. It was rarely abused... not this time, though. Lin you were right! Of course, you always are. God, should that be 'were'? Oh, I hate this! Suffice to say, the hotel saw no more of our custom during our stay. I wonder what the manager would have thought of that? It probably saved us a few bob in the end.

The craft fair was right up your street, darling. Lots of handmade items and there were some lovely wooden things crafted from drift wood. We settled on a little wooden star; it was a tea light holder, and very tactile. It resides in the summerhouse with our other travel mementos. I know you could have bought many other crafty items, but we were a bit tight on storage, so I breathed a sigh of relief. I was glad you didn't mention me buying a big power drill in the weekly offers at Lidl in Fort William! In the afternoon, we walked to the National Trust House and Gardens. The approach to it from the road went through a bird sanctuary in the corner of the Loch. There was a hide overlooking the beach, with posters of all the birds that could be seen and a wall chart score card for the breeds. We meandered up to the house through their exotic gardens. The place had a micro-climate, as many places on this coast do; the Gulf Stream, keeping the temperatures quite mild. The house had been used as a writing retreat by various authors over the years, and looking out over the Bay, I thought it would be a super place to put pen to paper and be inspired! The gardens were superb, but there was a lot of slopes and we were very aware of your hip pain. The sky was darkening, so we headed back to the road. Just before the bird hide, the heavens opened. We sheltered from the weather with the rain drumming on the roof. After twenty minutes there was a lull, so we ran for it – well, fast-walked, anyway! Five minutes from Brian, the rain washed in again and we were drenched. Never mind – a cosy meal in the van, with a bottle of wine and a DVD put the world back to rights. The next morning dawned bright and sunny, so we decided to get Brian ready to roll and explore. We drove down the south side of the loch, right next to the water, passing small farms and many sheep. There was even a guest house called Blue by Ewe! There were signs of derelict military establishments, one had been an anti-aircraft battery, and there was a very thought-provoking memorial to the horrendous Artic Convoys to Russia. This had been a loading area, a bleak, grey place to be leaving from. We traced our way back to Inverewe and headed north. We found more little villages and beautiful bays, but this was to be as far north as we ventured; it would keep for another time, we hoped.

We broke camp and readied Brian for the road. We were due to go to another site just south of Fort William, but I thought we'd seen a lot of this coast, so why not take the day to drive all up the north side of Loch Ness and book into the campsite halfway down the south side? Of course you agreed... You always did, even if you suspected it could be a dumb idea. We reached Fort Augustus in good time and stopped for a break, your blue parking badge saving us money yet again. We wandered up past the first couple of locks in the Caledonian Canal, which was a hive of activity. I noticed an hour-long boat tour was leaving shortly, so we played tourists and joined it. It was very scenic and interesting; apparently there's more fresh water in the depths of Loch Ness than in all the other lakes in Britain combined! Wow.

We had a pleasant drive around the loch. I was surprised, considering this was such a major attraction, that they'd let the land beside the water get so overgrown. A glimpse of the water was quite a rarity... such a shame, as this road could have been a real treat. The road along the south shore was far more narrow that the A-road to the north, though as long as people were considerate, it wasn't a problem. As we neared the campsite, an oncoming tractor hogged the centre of the road, forcing me into the rough ground alongside the carriageway. We were cursing as we pulled into the campsite. When I went to check in, a fellow camper remarked, "You know you have a flat tyre at the back?" Damn. We limped to our pitch, where I set about jacking up Brian and getting the spare out from under the rear end. Not an easy task! Having put the spare on, I examined the flat tyre. There was no obvious damage... then I saw the metal valve extension didn't look right. It was nearly snapped in two! After removing it, I used our powerful 12 volt pump to put air in the tyre, and it was right as bloody rain. I hadn't needed to change the wheel. Over a well-earned beer, that farmer's ears must have been burning! I certainly hope so.

Our pitch was in the centre of the site. That was okay, but there were some waterside spots, one of which became vacant next morning. I asked if we could move, and the answer was yes! Darling, you weren't too pleased to pack up and move, but we had two more days here and I had no intention of going off-site. Once we were set up, it was wonderful. We overlooked the water and the little beach with a jetty and boathouse; we could watch the tourist boats plying their trade, so the move was well worth it.

Soon, it was time to move on. Heading south toward Oban, we'd read about a seafood shack in the harbour and you were eager to try it. We stopped off at the big Morrisons in Fort William to resupply; chicken and bacon pasta bakes were becoming a favourite. We headed back towards Glencoe, but instead of going up the valley we turned right for the coast and Oban. Unfortunately, this took us past Bunree, the club site I'd cancelled to go to Loch Ness. You could have killed me! It was gorgeous, right on the seashore with fantastic views. Sorry Bongle, I cocked up again. Oban proved to be a traffic nightmare, the roads near the port were gridlocked and there was zero chance of finding a Brian-sized space. Backtracking, we managed to park a mile away on a residential street, so we put the kettle on and sat and watched the ferry leaving port heading for Mull. Our site for a couple of nights was happily quite lovely, set in the square of a country house's walled garden. When the warden heard you were nearly blind, she very kindly escorted you to the ladies' shower block, and explained where everything was.

The next day, we had a little explore on the pretty coastal road. There was a great bar overlooking the ocean, with lots of seafood on the menu – we had a super lunch, and l think I might have been forgiven. It was also on this stretch of coast that we added to our travelling family. Monk Monk, the small cute furry monkey I got you one Valentine's day, had travelled with us, sitting up on the dash looking over our route. We'd stopped for a coffee at a garden centre, our real reason for stopping being a car park big enough for Brian. Refreshed, we strolled around the garden aisles and then the shop... And there you spotted a friend for Monk Monk. Another cute monkey, shorter haired with a smiling chimp's face, of course we had to have him. Out on the road, the two 'boys' sitting together did seem a natural part of our travelling band. Our new friend wasn't as stable as Monk Monk and kept toppling over, so you christened him Naughty Morty!

After we swapped Brian for a caravan, the boys lived on a shelf in the summerhouse. They kept your ashes company for a year until you joined your beloved garden. The boys look sad, inevitably... I'm thinking that maybe I should take them on any road trips I do in the car. I digress a bit here... I do keep thinking about a motor home again, and I still get an MMM magazine now and then... But I read of huge site price increases, emission regulations, overcrowding and parking restrictions. I do love driving my hybrid Honda, so logically I should stick to road trips and hotels. That's cheaper, too, than a big outlay. Plus, I don't know if I'm fit enough for the camping life anymore.

Even though we never got to walk around Oban, or visit the fish shack (the town was just as rammed on our southward journey), we did have a very pleasant stay in the area. Now we were moving on towards Ayr and Argyll and Bute. While not as dramatic as the Highlands, it was looking to be a beautiful area. We moved to a site south of Ayr, adjacent to a rather impressive National Trust property called Culzean Castle. That was our destination for tomorrow, and it was easily walkable so Brian could stay put. Our lounge faced out to a small meadow, and past that to the sea. We had a pleasant evening in, with a nice meal, a bottle or two of wine, and a surprisingly good TV signal. Our aerial was a good one, raising a couple of feet above the roof on a mast. We turned it until the meter registered the strongest signal, and most of the time it worked a treat.

We'd been pretty lucky with the weather so far, and it continued. A gentle slope through a forest took us to the castle, which was in very good order. We wandered the battlements, taking in the views, hand-in-hand as always. We rarely bothered with interior rooms in Trust properties, as they were usually far too dark for you to see anything. You'd often tell me to go and look, but I didn't like to leave you sitting alone outside. I'd rather keep you company! Here though, some of the rooms were light and airy, so that made a nice change. We drew the line at venturing upstairs, though. A welcome coffee followed in the courtyard café, before strolling back to Brian. It was a nice day, and we had another fridge magnet as a reminder!

The next morning saw us getting ready to move again. We were quite excited about this move; a short hop to Garliestown, on a club site right in the harbour overlooking the sea. It was said there might even be seals! The drive took us through some interesting place names; Wigtown, and our favourite, Newton Stewart, a name that rolled off the tongue so well that we couldn't stop repeating it! Even the boys seemed to be laughing. Newton Stewart was the last sizable town before Garliestown, so we stopped at a large Co-Op. They seem to dominate Scotland in all the out-of-the-way places. Restocked, we carried on our journey, aware that we were in the final stages of this adventure. We arrived at the site around noon, way too early to check in as the clubs have strict rules on check in times. Logical, I suppose; you have to get units out before units come in, or the often small access roads would be gridlocked. We parked on a bit of tarmac opposite the camping ground. A sign read, Mobile Fish and Chip Van, Tuesday and Friday. Perfect, we were loving this place already! We wouldn't need to move Brian for the whole of our three-night stay. Hand-in-hand, we went to reception. I said, "I know we're too early to check in, but can we have an explore?" "Don't worry," the friendly warden said, "we don't worry about the rules around here too much. Have a look around, see which spot you fancy, then come and book in. It's pretty quiet at the moment." So we did. A stream ran through the property, dividing seasonal pitches on the town side from the touring ones by the water. A little bridge give access to the seasonal section. There was one space left overlooking the water, next to a number of caravans who looked set for long stays... We were lucky to have got here early. I finally found us an ideal spot. Parking up – backwards, of course – our comfy lounge looked out over the curve of the bay. We could see the pub and the path to the sandy beach at the other end of town... We would be very happy here. Tomorrow would be fish and chips from the van; tonight we'd splash out on a meal in the pub, so we needed to explore. From the site entrance, a right turn took us on a little path by the water, towards the pub. I noticed a house for sale overlooking the bay; a bit of a fixer-upper, but over the following weeks I looked at that house online several times. Only £70,000... a long way from Sussex, but oh so tempting. Between the path and the pub, The Harbour Inn, was an outdoor bowling green. We watched for a while, before carrying on to the beach. It was all so perfect. By the pub, a stream flowed out to join the bay, with the remains of an old watermill as a reminder of times gone bye. We had a couple of drinks in the bar and were pleased to see local mussels on the menu. With our table booked, we meandered back to Brian for a siesta before dinner. It was a lovely evening in the pub. The moules et frites were plump and tasty, in a creamy wine and lardon sauce. Very nearly as good as Brittany! We were so impressed that we booked a table for our last evening, as well. It being Pie Night might have been the persuader, though. We slept well in

Garliestown; the roof light open, the lapping of surf only feet away... very calming.

After breakfast, with our chores done, it was time to explore. Leaving the camp we turned left, towards the open sea, past the deeper water of the quayside where the remaining fishing boats moored and offloaded their catch every morning. Down a bramble-lined track around the headland, thoughtfully-provided benches allowed us to stop and sit hand-in-hand, watching the waves roll in and the gulls wheel overhead. I think if it wasn't for our mothers, we could have contemplated moving to this peaceful town. I collected our fish and chips from the van and we ate them under Brian's awning beside the sea. The next morning – our last here – we turned right at the gates, and followed the path past the bowling green and pub, to the start of the sandy beach. Modern flats or maisonettes enjoyed a sea view from the other side of the coast road. After that, scrubby woodland took over, and after rounding a curve in the road it felt like we could be miles from anywhere. Of course, we stopped for a pint on the way back. We could smell the pies for the evening cooking away. Dinner was as amazing as it had smelled at lunch time! We said goodbye to the landlords, who said, "Come back soon!" We wished it was that easy.

Packing up to move on the next morning, we really felt quite sad. This had probably been our favourite place on the whole trip. It had won a place in our hearts, and we said to ourselves we'd be back one day. Oh, how I wish that could be true, my darling.

We'd be heading towards England and home from now on. Being this far north, it would be crazy not to have a few days in the lake district. Windermere club site was about four hours away, passing Gretna Green and Carlisle again. Before

Gretna we passed signs for The Devil's Porridge museum. We were intrigued enough to look it up when we gained internet access; it was the site where gun powder and cordite was made for World War I armaments. It sounded like an horrendous place to work, not to mention rather risky. We wished we'd stopped for an hour or two. Kendal had a huge Morrisons, a nice change from Co-Ops, so we restocked. We hadn't used many main meals lately, but the wine was severely depleted! I spotted something called Chicken Donuts. I said to you, "They might be nice with salad..." But no. They were foul, and you didn't let me forget it! We topped up Brian's tank as well, and set off for the campsite. We chose a lovely pitch in a huge wooded site; they even had an on-site restaurant. Some of the caravans looked like they hadn't moved in years; the helpful receptionist said some folks lived on-site for the legal limit of nine months of the year, and went to Spain for the other three. The rates, including electricity, weren't bad, but I suspect that has all changed since Covid. We were very close to Bowness, so we wouldn't have to disturb Brian for the duration of our stay.

The next morning, after breakfast and the usual routine, we strolled into Bowness. A boat trip was our aim. A pleasant tour of Lake Windermere was over all too quickly, so we explored the town, which was busy with tourists even in the early season. We found a little bar-cum-bistro in a side street, and had a nice toasted sandwich with cheesy chips on the side. We walked around a little park close to the jetty, and found a hut overlooking the water where we sat awhile, before heading back to Brian. The next day we had a wander around town again, but by now we were eager to begin the journey home. We started to wonder what might greet us... interesting mail? An overgrown garden? New neighbours? Breakfasted and packed, it was time to go. It was a long drive;

in a car we'd probably have done it in a day, but with the van we decided on an overnight somewhere. Maybe the Cotswolds? Or Devizes, that nice site by the canal with a nice pub? We made good time, so it was Devizes, and one last pub meal. The next morning, it was just a two-hour hop. Back in 'Rusty Rustington' (as you used to say), things were as normal. The grass was a bit long, the weeds more prolific... and our first big adventure in Brian was over. Now came the unpacking, the laundry, the shopping... and then reloading Brian for our next outing together. With the 'boys' pointing the way, of course!

Our next big trip would be in September, after the school holidays. First to France, then down to Strasbourg, and exploring from there. During the summer we had a couple of trips, but stayed fairly close to home; Chichester, the New Forest, and Pevensey Bay. Just nice little midweek breaks, which we loved. Our wonderful garden was in full bloom, so we were loath to leave it for long during the height of its beauty. You'd spend the days in your beloved summerhouse, with occasional visitors, or listening to your talking books. If the weather was poor you would be at your crafting table in the office, painting or making birthday cards... Those were happy, glorious days. I would spend my days pottering about, with the van, the car, the garden and the cooking, I had plenty to occupy me. And of course, planning our French getaway. You always said that I enjoyed the planning almost as much as the travels! You were probably right; you always were. Those four years from 2016, when we stopped work, were the happiest of our lives. The camping trips, the cruises, and just living in wonderful Rusty Rustington. With our fantastic neighbours, and your WI ladies... it was a little piece of heaven. Until that horrific diagnosis, when our lives fell apart.

52

BRIAN GOES TO FRANCE

We embarked the ferry at Newhaven, for the four hour trip to Dieppe, as excited as children at Christmas. All being well, we should be on the road by 2pm local time. Just a couple of hours' drive to an Aire I'd picked out near Beauvais in Normandy. We'd brought a small picnic to have for lunch, along with a beer from the bar — just the one. It was a smooth crossing, and we were soon making our way back to Brian for our adventure to begin. Programming the sat-nav, we felt ready. It's such a joy driving in France, compared to the UK. The scenery passed by, meadows full of cattle that made us think about the wonderful cheeses we would get to sample. With glorious baguettes, too — nobody does bread like the French. Beauvais was on the way to our first main stop, a campsite on the banks of the Moselle. We couldn't wait. The sat-nav worked well, and took us directly to the Aire. These are little car parks in a great many towns in Europe, specifically for motorhomes. Some have full facilities and electric hook-ups; some are free, but most have a nominal charge. Ours just had water and a chemical toilet emptying point. The coin-operated ticket machine proved a bit troublesome, but I got it eventually. You were a little apprehensive, as the car park was not enclosed, but it was alongside a proper campsite and we did have a couple of neighbours. We settled in for a quiet night, just running on gas and 12 volt electrics. After the hectic first day, we actually slept very well. Packing up was easy and we set of for the Moselle — but not before stopping in the village for our first croissants and baguette of the trip. The campsite on the banks of the Moselle was quite lovely; a village was perched on the top of the hill behind us. It was a steep climb up — Google unfortunately does not convey height very well — but we were content with the riverside. Paths extended east and west, and would need exploring. The site had a terraced café and a super little shop where fresh bread and pastries could be ordered for the next morning. Brian was parked with the lounge looking out on the mighty river. Many wonderful hours were spent watching the craft wend their way into port. Huge barges passed, carrying all manor of cargo; even tractors and combine harvesters. The captain's car was usually perched on deck by the crane, waiting to be lifted to the shore for shopping trips and other tasks... Quite a nomadic life. The ship's dog would have the run of the deck, barking a greeting to other hounds heading the opposite way. We found it very tranquil and totally relaxing, we were really chilling out here. We had many strolls along the river, a pasta in the café one dinnertime, and always the evening bottle of wine sitting beside Brian. Our three nights here quickly passed without us leaving the site. Then it was time to move south, to Strasbourg, then on towards the pretty tourist hot spot of Colmar. Our next site was on the opposite side of the river to the town of Turkheim, wonderfully called Camping Medieval. The site was packed with vintage sports cars on trailers, as there was a rally in the hills on this weekend every year. We had a pitch with electricity booked, but not a specific one; we were told to drive around the site and find an empty place. Easier said than done, as many car trailers seemed to occupy spaces that should have been vacant pitches. Eventually, we found a space and settled in before going to explore. Turkheim was a beautiful, ancient town of pretty, chocolate box houses with geraniums cascading from countless window boxes. The imposing town hall sat beside a beautiful garden, with flower arches and benches to sit and take in the atmosphere. The cobbled streets were strangely at odds with the modern traffic vying for prized parking spaces. We sat a while taking it all in. As the sky was darkening, we found a supermarket — not immediately obvious from its medieval frontage. Stocked up, we headed for a pavement café, to sit under its awning as heavy raindrops started to patter down. Oh darling, it was so blissfully romantic, sitting watching people scatter as the rain came down. It would mean a second beer, before a break in the rain meant we could make a dash for it. This was a Saturday; tomorrow the cars would be competing, and it would be madness to try to take Brian out. So we had a quiet housework day, or should I say van-work day, followed by another stroll into town. It was quite lovely!

Monday dawned, and we were very excited. We had thought of going down as far as Annecy, and in hindsight we should have done, but that was a couple of hundred miles further south. So our destination was Camping Les Jonquilles, on the shores of Lac de Longemer, reached by a winding, scenic road through the region's low mountains. Fantastic, and even the weather was playing ball. At the western end of the lake was a small town. Google pinpointed a supermarket that we could re-provision at, along with a fuel station. It made sense to drive the mountain road without the weight of a full tank and larder. The route started out in the foothills, then we soon found ourselves winding up through the pine-clad slopes to a beautiful alpine town. Munster... of course, I started humming the TV show's theme tune. You asked if we could stop and have a wander; sadly, one of the negatives of being in a motorhome is that in tiny medieval villages, a large parking space is impossible to find. We said we'd come back, whilst secretly realising that we never would.

After Munster, the twisting road climbed to the top of the pass. On the way down we could see pretty Lac Longemer laid out before us. We headed to the main town at the western end, the one way system leading us to the fuel station and supermarket. Then, fully restocked, we set out for Camping Les Jonquilles on the south shore.

Reception housed a well-stocked shop and a pizza café. It sat on the main road around the lake, with the campsite tumbling down a slope to the lake shore. As it was out of season, there were some motorhome pitches available right by the cool, clear waters; or, we could be up the slope nearer to the café. The facilities for bathing and the usual chores were halfway up the hill. Of course, we decided a waterside spot would be best, although I think the fact that I would be doing most of the walking for the chores made it an easy choice for you! With Brian nose-first to a small embankment, our lounge faced the lake, a stone's throw away across the access road. There was even a small, grassy space where we could put our table and chairs directly on the bank! It was like our own little private bit of heaven.

Across the water, younger, fitter people paddled canoes and paddleboards. To the right we could see a waterside café, with tables on staging above the water. That would be our lunchtime objective for tomorrow. A happy thought to end a wonderful day on! Sleep came easily in the wonderful mountain air, with our windows open — after lights out, of course, to keep the bugs out! I suspect that few people really appreciate the high design level of motorhomes. The windows for instance; not only do you have blinds or curtains for nighttime, but also mesh fly screens that can be pulled across when the windows are open. Amazing what they squeeze in. Next morning, after our usual two cups of tea with biccies and a read, we set about the household chores. You stayed van-side while I trekked up the hill with the rubbish, recycling, and to empty the toilet — admittedly, I was the one that filled it most! After two trips I was ready for a shower. Being a cool, calm lady, you elected to have a wash in Brian, while I trekked back up the hill again. At least our large onboard water tank was good for a few days; we used a separate three-litre container for the kettle, just to be safe, and bottled water for drinking and squash. We were lucky with the weather darling; sunny days and balmy evenings. We had a lovely day planned, a gentle walk around the western end of the lake to the waterfront café. The hardest part was the slog up to reception and the road. After that, the roadside path wended down through woods strewn with picnic benches. We passed another camping ground, which had more facilities; a clubhouse, and entertainment — more of a holiday park. "Not for us," I grumpily said. You said you were very happy with our tranquil lakeside spot. We were lucky enough to nab the last table on the decking above the water. With beers ordered, we perused the menu; sadly no lake trout, as it was more snack orientated. But you did have a nice pasta, and of course I went for the burger! After a second beer, and of course a visit to the toilets, we strolled back to Brian. The slope up to reception seemed much steeper than it felt on the way down! We relaxed by the lake, you engrossed in your beloved talking books while I studied the map for the next leg of our adventure.

We were missing the sea, and you had a real hankering for seafood. I must admit, some fresh Moules et Frites would go down well. If we headed more or less straight west, we'd hit southern Brittany somewhere around Pornic. That had been on our wish list for some time. I found a site around the halfway mark, next to a reservoir. Where exactly I can't recall, but it was just a single night to break up the journey. As always on a travelling day we were up early, showered and on the road by nine. Cereal would see us through until a supermarket stop to stock up, refuel and hopefully find a nice snack for lunch.

The snack shacks in France are very overpriced, and it is mainly chips on the menu. Instead, we stopped at a boulangerie and bought wonderful bread and pastries, with some delicious cheese from the fridge. The campsite beside the huge reservoir was very modern, with large pitches, a super shower block and a snack bar. We set up camp and wandered over to the water. A bar could be seen in the distance, so we headed off for a quiet beer. It was very peaceful. I think the beers were Leffes, one of our favourites; I got some crisps to nibble, and we enjoyed a couple of hours watching the fitter youngsters at their water sports.

The next morning we set off west. The autoroutes go mainly north-south, so we were on scenic A-roads which was very pleasant. Hitting the coast in the Pornic area, we soon found that any site close to the sea was full. We eventually found one a little way inland. It was more or less a concrete car park set on a hill, but it did have a distant sea view. Not much to walk to, so it would just be one night. Linda, darling, you had the great idea that perhaps we should go up to the more familiar northern Brittany... As it turned out, simply brilliant. Just north of Pornic is a stunning bridge spanning the Loire estuary, saving a long drive to Nante. The views from the bridge were fabulous; such a shame that we couldn't stop and take photos. From the far bank we struck north-east, to see where we would hit the coast. Campsites abounded, so we could not see a problem. I can picture it still, but exactly where I can't be certain; of course, you would recall it, my darling.

I think it was around Kernic, that we found a bay with paths by the sea and restaurants overlooking the water. Half a mile to east there was a campsite on the beach, so off we went. The site was full, but they said we could spend one night in the overflow pitches beside the access road overlooking the bay. So no facilities, but that wasn't a problem for us for one night in Brian. It was only ten minutes to town, so I said, "Let's push the boat out and have a nice seafood meal!" You didn't need much persuading, dearest! We chose a place with an upstairs terrace, with views over the bay. We could even see Brian resting in the distance. Of course, we both chose the Moules ala Brittany, with lardons, cream and cider. There was no sign of the waiter, so I went in to order. We needed a bottle Muscadet to get things going, and I had a surprise to spring. The waiter returned with the crisp white wine in a chiller sleeve… and a tray of a dozen oysters! Oh Bongle, the look on your face! You were overwhelmed. I said, "Well, you always said you wanted to try them, so where better?" I think I had four. They weren't bad, but not really my thing. You said they were lovely, and with a squeeze of lemon, delicious. I hope you were telling the truth! There was no need to guess with the moules, they were delicious! We wandered back to Brian for a second bottle of wine, while watching the waves lapping the bay. I patted myself on the back for remembering to switch the fridge over to run on gas when we parked up. Come the morning we were homeless again. I said, "Let's just head east on the coast road and see what we find." We did, and boy did we fall on our feet! On a little peninsula by a tiny hamlet was a slice of heaven, a small Dutch-owned site whose pitches were on the point of land and surrounded by the sea in a horseshoe shape. In the centre was a small pool and a bar café. We'd stocked up at a supermarket in Kernic, and could even do some laundry; there was a shed in the car park with machines and dryers, what a bloody good idea! Then we followed the small coastal B-road hoping, to find an out-of-the-way campsite. We did; we arrived about 1pm, to find reception closed. A sign just told us to find an empty pitch and they would see us later. The spacious pitches were all divided by low hedges. No.7 was empty and had commanding sea views. The site was run by two lovely young Dutch girls on behalf of a Dutch camping organisation. We had four wonderful nights here to round off our trip. We didn't take Brian out at all; there were footpaths around the headland for us to explore, and I had the pool to myself whenever I wanted a dip. You were content to sit in the sun with your talking books. The little café, also staffed by the girls, had a very limited menu, but we wanted to support them at lunchtimes. Our favourites — crazy I know, in a land abounding in grand fare — were crispy pancakes! Just like Birds Eye crispy pancakes of old, filled with ham and melted cheese, served with chips and sliced baguette. All too soon, our four nights were over. We had to hot foot it back to Dieppe, with just a transit stop in a large complex on the way. Little did we know this was to be Brian's last big adventure, but boy, it was a good one!

NORWAY AND ICELAND, SEPTEMBER 2023

Well darling, another cruise; Iceland this time, which was always high on our wish list. I know it will be very scenic. I've booked a couple of excursions this time, but sixteen nights on Arcadia... I know it's a mistake, even now on day two. It's 30th August and the weather is rubbish; cloudy and grey, and it looks set to continue for the next two weeks, so not much chance of seeing the Northern Lights. It's just not the same without you by my side, Linda. The cabin is nice enough, and again I will only use the buffet. The big negative for me is they've changed the wine list, and not for the better. There used to be a very passable mid-priced French Sauvignon Blanc, called Holy Snail. I know sounds revolting, but what is revolting is its replacement! They're even in the process of using up the Thatchers Gold cider and replacing it with cheap and chemical-tasting Strongbow. Cruising with P&O is really not luxury travel anymore. The saving grace is the two daily lectures on sea days. This morning it was about the inner planets of our solar system; this afternoon's is on photography, how to take a better picture, which was particularly useful. Even the roulette is losing its appeal. I think this cruise is too close to the last one to the Baltic. I seem to be running around like a headless chicken! I think I desperately need your negligence case to be put to bed, so I can move on and properly plan for my remaining time in this life. Hate it, hate it, hate it.

It's black tie night tonight, so I will probably watch a film after a couple of gins. There used to be a movie selection available on the TVs, but that has gone now too, leaving just a few crappy channels. There are dozens of DVDs in the library, but no obvious way to view them! I know I sound like (and probably am) a grumpy, ungrateful old curmudgeon, but I really just can't find anything that gives me happiness. Sorry, darling, but that is the way of it. I found out the DVDs are for suite guests, so to hell with it, I splashed out £252 for satellite internet. I'm much happier now! I can use Facebook, check emails, watch Amazon Prime and Netflix, and even catch-up TV. I told myself that stopping the casino will fund it; so far, so good. Today we are in Skjolden at the end of Sognefjond fjord, Norway's longest at 153 miles. It's very beautiful, or it would have been if we didn't get here by night! Hopefully I'll see some of it if we leave before sunset. Got some nice photos. The camera is pretty good, and I eventually learned how to transfer the pics to the phone so they can go on Facebook and WhatsApp. Otherwise, nobody would get to see them. Tomorrow, I have a little boat trip to a waterfall, which should be exciting. But even that got changed from 1pm to 9.30am. Nothing seems to go to plan here, now. Even the shows; there are no nice theatre productions, so far it's been The Two Tenors twice! Needless to say I didn't bother. Even the food now is decidedly third-rate. It can't just be me, can it? I'm sitting here now by the indoor pool, trying to write as men with hammers are smashing hell out of the opening roof... I'm going to move down to the pub, now. P&O, you suck!

A slight diversion; I moved down to the pub and they're playing Queen, which is good move. A guy at the next table was having a pint when his wife returned. She put her arms around his neck to give him a hug, and he shrugged her off. I wanted to scream, "No, you fool! You don't know how precious hugs are!" But of course I didn't, he looked a bit tough!

We're in Alesund today, dear. We had a wonderful coach tour here in 2018, remember? Out around the little islands, the church, that super little bridge and the café on the windy headland by the red and white lighthouse. Today I went on a boat trip, a modern catamaran with plush leather seats. Coffee, waffles and jam were thrown in; we've had that before on a boat trip. The voyage was very scenic, but the waterfall at the end was disappointing, a mere dribble compared to the gushing waters we saw on our trip. On the way back I used my phone to take the photos off the camera and put some on Facebook and some on WhatsApp for Hunny. She's never joined the ranks of social media like your other old friends. We keep in touch most days; your old Cream Teas group is still intact, just missing yourself, my dearest girl. This place brings back so many memories. We'll reach Iceland after a couple of boring sea days. That's new territory for me; a shame the weather is turning grey and wet from tomorrow.

As we left Alesund the weather really closed in. The captain announced that we were headed into a storm for the next two days, so the pools have been emptied and the outside decks closed. It was a bit rough in the night; I rolled out of bed and got jammed by the wall! You would have laughed your socks off as I shuffled out! It's rocking and rolling still today, with another sea day to go before Reykjavik. The morning lecture was on the Apollo missions and the afternoon one about Vikings — both very interesting, and no doubt the day's highlight. The cabaret tonight is Maurice Grumbleweed... Need I say more? Lunch was yet another roast, which they can't cook at all. I'll watch something on Netflix tonight. I'm enjoying reading again though, so that's a bonus. Not fancying yet more rubbish from the buffet, I made myself a little picnic of beef and ham rolls and took it to the cabin for later. I already have some Pringles in the room, so I bought a bottle of Merlot red wine to go with it. It was just about palatable. I had my usual pink gin and Fevertree tonics in the East bar, way up on Skydeck 11. It was so rough and windy that the spray was hitting the windows right up there! It was quite mesmerising as we rolled about, and a bit draughty, too. After two days without roulette I did have a go, and turned £60 into £50! Then back to the room for my picnic in front of Antiques Roadshow, followed by an episode of Lucifer on Netflix on my tablet. Not the double dose of cabarets we used to enjoy on Ventura in the good times, eh darling? I shouldn't be too negative about this cruise, as the others seem to be enjoying it regardless of the weather and cost cutting. I know it's just me; I can't find pleasure in anything, and seem to live in perpetual self-torment.

The captain put a bit of a spurt on, and by early morning we got to leeward of the east of Iceland. We're now cruising slowly anticlockwise around northern Iceland, to be in Reykjavik for the morning. We'll stop there for two days. The lectures today were at 10 and 11, the first an overview of Iceland, the second on volcanoes, on earth and in space. They've been the highlight of the trip for me, I hope there will be more. Having both talks in the morning does make for a rather long rest of the day, though. I had a cooked breakfast today, not having had dinner last night. The buffet was heaving at lunchtime, so I just had a burger and fries, eaten standing up as tables were scarce. After a circuit of the deck to blow away the cobwebs, I went down to the pub where I am writing this with a pint of Morretti lager. I cashed in the £50 of casino chips, but did succumb to a set of bingo cards for 4.15pm to pass some time. These are the first ones on this cruise... my, I am being good! In port tomorrow for two days the casino will be shut, which is no bad thing. I'm told there's a shuttle bus while we're there, which will be good. It'll be nice to explore somewhere new. I bloody wish you were here, though. Bugger. The sun did come out briefly today, but now the clouds have closed in again for the day. I keep looking at the white wave tops, hoping to spot a whale... God, how many hours have we wasted doing that over the years? I expect tonight will be a repeat of last night — except for the roulette. Well, unless I get really bored...

We're in Reykjavik today! We're berthed at the commercial port, thirty minutes from the tourist hotspots. We're opposite the small island of Videy, a pretty little uninhabited place with a small jetty and a charming white wooden house. It is also home to the Imagine Peace Tower, a laser light memorial to John Lennon from Yoko. Sadly, it only turns on from John's birthday, 9th October, to his assassination day in November. That's a shame, as I would have had the perfect view from my balcony. I did get off today, around noon, but the queue for the shuttle was huge and there are no toilets on the dock. I was scared I'd get caught out waiting to get back aboard, so I bottled out. What a wreck I've become! Instead, I had a walk on the top deck. They've been hosing down the balconies today, the one time there was a couple of hours' sunshine! I had my first nice meal though, a moussaka and salad from the buffet. Tonight they do a Chinese, so it might be two good meals in one day... Wow, we shall see. While sitting here, writing in the 'Intermezzo' lounge on deck three, I've been online looking at taxis. From what I can work out it's about £12 from the ship to the city centre, so to hell with it, I will go for that tomorrow after a light breakfast. For the rest of the day, reading and watching Lucifer on Netflix will have to do.

Well Bongle, I worked up the courage to go ashore today. I'm starting to think I go on these trips as a form of self-punishment. Don't ask! With you it was all so different, we used to love these adventures and seeing new places. Rekjavik Iceland, always high on our wish list, was not so great on my own. I'd worked out that a taxi should be around £12 into town, to avoid the bus queues. I got off at 10.30am and there was one taxi on the rank, a Honda CRV. I took that as a good omen. I asked the driver to take me to the famous church; from there I could walk through town to the promenade. Two girls appeared at the rank, and I said I would take them to town. There were no more cabs, so they gratefully accepted. Turns out they were crew, so I was happy to pay. It was 3500 IKR, around £20, but so much easier; I doubt I could have walked up to the church from the seafront bus stop. The towering church was very impressive from outside, looking like a stalagmite that had been drawn or dragged up out of the ground. Inside it was surprisingly plain; except for the magnificent organ, everything was just grey. Walking down through town to the prom, I noted there were no prices on display in the shops — so as not to frighten off the tourists, I guess. Many of the houses were made from sheet metal, although I suspect the insulation would be superb. On a street corner a bride and groom were kissing, but with no sign of family or guests, which I found very strange.

Down on the seafront I walked to the famed Sun Voyager, a life-size steel skeleton of a Viking Longship. Although bizarrely, the sculptor insists that it is NOT a Viking Longship. In sunshine it would have been magnificent. I walked east towards the huge concert hall by the city harbour, which is the drop-off point for the shuttle bus, and has a café with rare public toilets. As I approached, I could see an empty taxi rank, but as luck would have it a port shuttle bus pulled in beside me. After we'd passed the Sun Voyager on the right, overlooking the ocean was a nondescript white wooden house. This was were Reagan met with Gorbachev, and the cold war began to thaw... Now that should have been the site for the Imagine Peace beacon! So apt, but I guess it was too close to the airport. Fifteen minutes later I was walking up the gangplank. I'd been gone just ninety minutes, but I had seen and photographed everything on my wish list. Great! Mission accomplished.

Last night we cruised around to Isafjordur. The itinerary made it look like a day of scenic cruising, but no — just like on the Canaries cruise, the scenery passes at night. The town proved to be a nice experience, even though it's quite industrial, and there's a huge building site beside the ship. A few minutes' walk opposite the ship is another small harbour, which has the town's museum. On the way there is a microbrewery, with a café attached. I didn't go into the museum as it was dark, cramped and overrun with tourists, but behind it was a quayside with a large trawler and a small beach where water sports could be enjoyed. Windsurfers, kayaks and a couple on paddleboards were taking to the chill waters... of course, they all had wet suits. Across the bay, curving roads wound up into the mountains. Iceland looks a seriously good place for a road trip. We're moored in a deep cleft, or fjord, between two mountains, meaning the ship's satellite internet and phones are out of action. No Netflix this afternoon! I'm getting Lucifer withdrawals. Luckily, the mobile has a good signal, so I got some nice pictures on Facebook. You would have liked it here, darling, it's so quiet and peaceful. I stopped for a beer at the brewery; not too bad, at £8 for a half-litre. I sat outside, and a lady asked if she could sit down. We chatted, and an elderly American lady asked me what the beer was like. "Very good," I said. Her husband was on a walker and she wanted to find somewhere he could have a beer. We all started chatting. She was from Colorado, and migrants became the topic of conversation. Rachel, the first lady to join me, was from Perth. She said Australia had got it right, and we all agreed. The American lady said I could join them for dinner if I wanted company… a shame she's on the Norwegian Line ship! They moved on, and Rachel and I talked some more. She's a tour guide here, and got locked down here during covid. Luckily, her husband came to visit her just before lockdown. Now they live here, and they love it. The only concern is that the nearest hospital is a few hours away in Reykjavik. I told her your sad tale, my dearest, and that earned me a hug. She said she's going to Latvia for a holiday in October, and has booked to go to a shooting range to fire an AK 47! It was quite an interesting day. I have a trip out tomorrow, which should be pretty good.

I'll admit that I was apprehensive about today's coach trip. Cramped seats, and no toilets for hours… but the views more than made up for the discomfort. The day started well by being in quite an attractive port called Akureyri. My balcony looked out on a small waterfall beside the main road across the fjord. Kayakers paddled near its tumbling waters, which I later learned were warm from thermal activity. Apparently, sometimes ready-cooked salmon come tumbling over! The coach was due to leave at 1.15pm. I breakfasted at 9am and didn't eat again until evening, playing it safe. A mid-morning coffee was my only drink. The coach was virtually full, but the back seat was empty. Two other large gentlemen joined me a few minutes later. The seats were tiny, the seat belt anchor was stuck in my butt! As for doing it up, no chance! My idea of hell, dear. I contemplated getting off. Godafoss waterfall was 45 minutes away. After that, we were supposed to tour through the old town, go to the botanic gardens, and be back at the ship and all aboard by 4.30pm. A bit tight! So when the coach broke down at 1.30pm, in the middle of nowhere, my worst fears were realised. The driver banged and crashed in the engine bay beneath our seat, then gave up and requested another coach. At 2.10pm it arrived, an old bus which was even more cramped and noisy. We got dropped in the Godafoss car park about 2.40pm and were told we could walk along the tumbling river to the main falls. But we must be back on the bus, which would move to the café complex by 3.18pm! The poor folk who were not quick walkers would not make it to the main event and back in time; indeed, some elected to stay on the bus. How sad! I strode as quickly as I could to the main viewpoint. The thundering, twelve-metre-high horseshoe-shaped cascade was majestic. Spray filmed my camera lens, but the pictures were superb, and well worth the trip. I made it to the café in time for a much-needed pee, and I bought a bottle of water and a chocolate bar as there was no beer on sale. Back on the coach, we took the direct route back to town, and did indeed go through gaily-coloured streets of wooden houses on our way to the gardens. We passed a huge outdoor swimming pool complex, steaming from the warm thermal water. Oh God, how I would have loved to go in. Our tour guide had spoken to the ship, so we could be fifteen minutes late at maximum. We were allotted twenty-eight minutes in the gardens. Through the gates there were a few flowers and colourful winter cabbages. I thought of picking some for the chef, to have with the roasts, instead of the never-ending mixed veg! I saw the café and reckoned a beer and another pee before the queues would be the best use of fifteen minutes. It was lovely beer! We got back just after 4.30pm, along with another coach. Of course, P-and-bloody-O only had one gangway set up. Ominous black clouds were looming on the horizon. Spots of heavy rain started, and a hundred and thirty people, mainly pensioners, with several on walkers and in wheelchairs, waited to go through security and an x-ray in the safest, most peaceful country in the world. Get real, P&O!

Back on board, I headed for a bar. I wanted to get my photos off the camera, into the phone and onto Facebook and WhatsApp, for all the people at home eagerly (I hope!) waiting for them, before we left phone signal range. Keeping my coat and camera, just in case any whales showed up, I went to the buffet, where I devoured lasagne and salad. I then went up to the Skydeck's east bar for my evening gin and tonics. I then retired to my cabin for a couple of glasses of Merlot and Netflix... all in all, a good day. Next we have two sea days, so I doubt there will be anything to report until we reach Edinburgh.

On Saturday, our first sea day, I mainly read and watched Lucifer. I did go to the two lectures, which were a nice distraction. The captain had a cocktail party for loyalty members, so after my gins in the east bar I went to the party, just to hand my ticket in for the draw. The receptionist was aghast when I turned and walked away... Perhaps if you'd been here, my dear? The second sea day looked to be the same. I went to the theatre in the morning, but could only take two minutes. They've turned the heating on in a bloody heatwave! This completed my misery, and crowns my new loathing of P&O. I tried the afternoon talk, with the same result; it seems my next three days are probably going to be spent in my cabin. As the cruise nears an end, the buffet food is becoming even more dire. The three steps to heaven on the back railing are looking quite good. I seem to be going into a darker place, instead of coming to terms with this existence. I'm giving the lawyers until your second anniversary to reach resolution; if not, I intend to bombard the press. 'Repeated NHS Blunders Kill Blind Queen's Guider!' An eye catching headline! Revenge and justice is starting to be a priority. If I top myself as well, it will ensure publication. I had to let that out. I wonder if I'll delete it in time? But not now. As I said, a dark, dark place.

It's Edinburgh tomorrow. Well, actually the middle of the river near Edinburgh. The queues for the tenders will be horrendous, so that's not for me. But I do hope I can get some good photos from the top deck. I was pleasantly surprised by the views of the bridges and estuary. As the clouds lifted I could just make out the castle about five miles away. My great new camera even managed to capture it on full zoom. Otherwise though, it was a very long day aboard.

We reached Newcastle today, although I think we are in South Shields docks. It's not very scenic, but there's a small yacht marina and a nice café by the gangway. I had a walk around, admiring the boats. Is that the ultimate escape, maybe? A couple of lovely pints of Aspalls cider, sitting overlooking the boats, was nice. It's another long sea day tomorrow, except there will be packing to do. I hope my departure from this cruise is as efficient as it was last time; I can't wait to drive my car and get home.

54

REVELATIONS

Whether this script will ever see the light of day, or publication, I don't know. I hope so, as perhaps others in the same lamentable situation might gain some comfort from it. Wonderful as it has been to recount our adventurous life together, it has also been self-tormenting. Going on cruises and trips like the ones we used to so enjoy is not working without you, it's almost a form of self-punishment. I'm having thoughts that my whole existence is just trying to recapture what has been lost; the flat, the garden... it will never be the same. Should I enter some kind of nomadic existence and just disappear? I think few would really miss me, if they're truthful. I just really don't know. But changes have to be made for my remaining life to have any merit.

Coming back to our home and garden this time, it really hit me that there is nobody waiting to greet me. The neighbours, of course, are wonderful, but I've had no calls from family as yet. It just proves that you were my whole world, dearest Linda.

WELSH ROAD TRIP, OR ESCAPE?

October, that dreadful and dread month, has rolled around again. Two long years, my darling, and it doesn't get any easier. I thought a trip away in my lovely Honda might provide a bit of a boost — just seven nights, so I can run for home if I'm away for too long. So, on Tuesday 3rd October, after the food bank collection run in Chichester, I set off for Andover, a jumping-off point for the adventure. Of course, being me it could not go like clockwork. On the Chichester run the car started having a wobble. Occasionally the steering would give a little 'shimmy,' as if the road was worn with tramlines caused by heavy trucks. Also, the steering warning lamp would flash up for a second. This happened four or five times in that twenty mile trip. After dropping off the provisions, I tried to get to my local Honda dealer, hoping they could just check out the steering on a ramp. I couldn't get there, as the road was down to one lane again; those never-ending road works on the A259! Three long years, and still they frig around with it! I came home and loaded the car. To hell with it, I would make for Andover, and if the issue persisted I could abort the trip in the morning. All the rooms were paid for, so there was nothing to gain by aborting. The problem persisted, but I noticed two little sets of letters were also lit on the dash. Were they always there? There's so much going on in the dashboard on this hi-tech beastie, I really didn't know. 'ACC' and 'LKAS'... I assumed the first was for air-conditioning, except it wasn't on. It was 1pm, so I decided I would stop at the Scotney services for a Big Mac. We used to love starting our driving adventures with a Sausage and Egg Mc Muffin meal! I took the handbook in with me. The burger proved rather tasteless, but the handbook was a revelation! ACC was Cruise Control. That wasn't on as I never mastered it; too damn complex, especially with the addition of a speed limiter. No way I wanted to let that beast loose! LKAS was the answer. 'Lane Keeping Automatic Steering!' What nut job came up with that? If you were doing endless trips on a motorway, the cameras would nudge the steering should you drift near a lane marker line, ie, fall asleep! How it got turned on I do not know, but with it turned on if you changed lane or overtook a car it would try to keep you in lane. ARGH! I soon read how to disable it, and never again will it be switched on. Darling, I know you would have been laughing fit to burst at my stupidity. And rightly so! Perhaps I should get an old Ford Cortina, or something that is as low-tech as I am.

So I found myself on the outer fringes of Andover. With the car, I can get annual updates for Evie's sat-nav. I hadn't gotten around to updating the thing, as it's quite complex. Of course, Andover has lots of new building work and junctions... where hasn't, down south? So getting to the White Hart Inn was a tad stressful, with a pint required on arrival. The Marston Inn was a little run down, as was the town centre; like many, it is dying on its feet. I checked in. My second floor room was tired but clean, and the bed comfy. Google had said that there was a Viking Longship in the river close to the Inn, so I went exploring. It was indeed a Longship, but just the outline of one and its crew in wrought iron. A bit of an anticlimax. I spent a quiet evening, with gammon and chips for dinner. They did have a nice wine, though, a New Zealand Marlborough. I just had basic bacon and eggs for breakfast, as I didn't want to be too full on a traveling day. I was excited to see Ironbridge. Andover was just as hard to get out of as it had been getting in; the town centre was a ghost town, even at 8.45am, but the peripheral was manic! I didn't want to go via Birmingham, so tried the route through Kidderminster and Bridgnorth instead. Apart from a short bit on the M5, it was a very relaxing cross-country trip.

Ironbridge did not disappoint. I put the south-side car park's postcode into Evie's sat-nav, finding it just a stone's throw from the bridge. Pay and display of course... Oh darling, we didn't realise what a godsend your blue disabled badge was! I certainly miss it at times. I do still use it at Tesco, when shopping for the old ladies, but would never use it where the registration number might be checked. Even that only runs until April 2024; then yet another facet of you will have to be put away. Nobody asked for it back, so I didn't want to part with it. It seems like a connection, somehow. I strolled to the bridge, where a toll house sits on this side. A sign displayed the charges from the last century, even a price for cattle and sheep! It was a privately owned bridge, so even the military had to pay. It's a masterpiece of engineering, and looks as good as new; it was quite busy with tourists, but not overly so. There are walks along the river to either side. I went far enough to get some nice photos, then went and sat outside the hotel on the north bank with a pint, and put my black hat on for a while. You would have been bowled over by the place, my darling, and doubtless we would have stopped for lunch. Food doesn't play a big part in my travels, these days. I stopped in a supermarket on the way here, so back in the car I had a chicken wrap and a bag of crisps. My hotel, the Water Rat Inn, was only a mile down the road, so I still had time to kill. I thought a visit to the Victorian Town Museum would be good, on the outskirts of Ironbridge. Surprisingly it was a paid car park, but then everything is, now. You got ten minutes free, and after that it was very expensive per-hour rate. Luckily, I decided to look at ticket prices before paying for the car park. £23.50 for adults and pensioners! Bloody hell, I only wanted to kill an hour or two. No way, so I scooted off quick within my ten free minutes' use of their valuable tarmac! How the hell can families afford to go out for the day? To justify those costs you'd need to spend a day at each museum, and in this town there are several! But enough of Mr Grumpy for now. My hotel was a pleasant surprise; a modern wooden extension for the bar and restaurant adjoining a large Victorian house, which was the B&B block. I sat with a pint while doing a bit of writing, overlooking the lawn with tables leading down to the river Dee. A Weeping Willow stood to my right, and another cast iron bridge lay off to the left, carrying the railway line this time. My room was modern and comfortable, with a throw and scatter cushions on the bed which I immediately scattered onto the floor on the far side of the bed! How pointless! On the downside, my bathroom was up a flight of stairs in the attic. Bugger, for this old boy that was going to be a big issue in the night, so I grabbed my big emergency bottle from the car. Problem solved! The TV had Netflix, so I logged in, happy knowing I could continue my Lucifer box set. How sad! Down in the restaurant, I was pleased to see they also had a Marlborough wine, so I splashed out on a duck breast for dinner. It was superb, followed by a coffee and brandy, just like our old travelling days. No, my darling, don't bring Cognac up again, please! A comfortable night was followed by superbly cooked poached eggs on toast with bacon, always a good test of a cook. All in all, it was a nice stay.

I had a relaxing sixty-mile drive into Wales next, with a supermarket stop to stock up in Shrewsbury. Not too many road works so far, but I'm not sure if a mobile speed camera got me on a 30mph road that ought to be 40! I was taking a slightly longer route to see a couple of places in Llangollen, just over the border. When I crossed the border it was still only 11.30am. Seeing a National Trust sign, I thought a coffee stop was in order. The sign led me to Chirk Castle, perched on a hilltop above the car park. There was a shuttle bus to take people to the top, but I headed for the toilets to be safe. I still can't pass one by, my dear! Of course, the bus had departed during those three minutes. I surprised myself by managing the climb; a handy bench after the steepest part was most welcome. There wasn't a great deal to see. The gardens were past their best, but the view was good. I had a hot chocolate, always our favourite at National Trust places.

I wanted to get some pictures of the Pontcysyllte Aqueduct, but for some reason the car park postcode wasn't recognised. I thought, it can't be that hard to find. In the event I caught a glimpse in the distance, but never spotted a turning for this popular attraction. It didn't help having a forty-ton articulated truck up my exhaust pipe! The Chain Bridge Hotel was my destination for lunch; I'd found it online, unfortunately just after I'd booked my accommodation for this trip. Just to the west of Llangollen, it sits on a spit of land jutting out into the water like a finger. The tumbling rocky rapids of the river Dee rushes by on the south side of the hotel en route to Ironbridge. The Chain Bridge provided a perfect platform for photos. The tranquil Llangollen Canal passes on the north side of this exceptional hotel. I've got to come and stay in this family-run establishment, preferably in the cold, frosty months. I had a nice chat with the young barmaid, mainly moaning about the countrywide speed restrictions that will, I'm sure, put a dent in tourist numbers. There was a group of oriental ladies who enquired what river this was, and a hen party staying at the hotel, awaiting a minibus taxi. They were taking selfies on the bridge, so of course I offered to take a few group ones for them. In the end, I only had two pints of a very nice local cider. I wasn't hungry after the super poached eggs I had for breakfast. So, off to Bala and my chalet. I wasn't supposed to get in before 4pm, but I thought I would find it and see the lay of the land. I was behind a motorhome for some miles, and was amazed when it took the same tiny turning I did to get to my chalet. I found my place and looked to see if it seemed ready. The key wasn't in the key safe, but the door was unlocked with the key in it. The place was clean and smelled of the anti-Covid misting fog they used. I didn't know what to do, but thought surely they won't mind if I put my shopping in the fridge? I noticed the motorhome parked in the yard of the big farmhouse adjoining my chalet, and wondered if they were part of the host family. I hung around a few minutes, then thought, to hell with it, it's 3pm! So I unloaded the car. In the event, nobody came – not for the whole of my stay, as it happens. The inside of the chalet was superb; modern and comfortable, the smart TV even had Amazon Prime and Netflix pre-loaded!

I passed a quiet night with microwave pasta and a bottle of wine. I was a bit miffed that the chalet booking details didn't mention the oven; I'd just brought microwave meals. Never mind, I was hoping to have lunch out most days. Today, my first full day dawned grey and drizzly... Of course it did, this is me! It seemed pointless to try going up into the mountains when sun was forecast after today for this region. Inevitably, back home was an Indian summer and a mini-heatwave! The nearest coastal town was Barmouth. Not without its memories, eh Bongle? About twenty miles away, it would be a nice, scenic drive. Luckily there weren't too many 20mph sections... those new restrictions are a pain in the backside on long high streets. After a pleasant drive to the coast, I paid for two hours' parking and had a wander in the mist and murk, before getting a pensioners' discount on my fish and chips. I sat in the car, eating while watching the odd dog walker on the beach. It was very quiet. I didn't even have a pint; this evening was a repeat of the previous one. The next day was Saturday. I planned to spend it up in the high mountains, and maybe get all the way to Snowdon and the tourist hot spots. The promised sun had yet to show, though. After cereal and a bit of Marmite on toast, I was ready to hit the road. I was looking forward to this; Evie might even get put in sports mode. A few hundred yards from my little village, just over the bridge into Bala, a B-road led up into the mountains towards Blaenau Ffestiniog. The first few miles were lovely; I wound up the narrow road, and passed over a cattle grid after which sheep wandered aimlessly. I turned sports mode off and dropped my speed down to 20mph. At a scenic reservoir, I pulled off the road into a small farm entrance and walked back with the camera. The farm had a pig pen, with a single huge pot-bellied pig the sole resident! We exchanged a grunt or two... so at least I spoke to someone today! The views were good, but a bit of sunshine would have made them stunning. Damn, the BBC weather report is never right. Back in Evie, I went higher into the mountains. Suddenly, a curtain of fog and low cloud came down, slowing me to a crawl because of the sheep. I drove for thirty minutes, and as I got higher, the visibility worsened. I hit a junction; my options were to go higher into the soup, or turn left to Harlech, on the coast. Left it was! Back on the coast, the sun was actually out, so the scenic road from Harlech to Barmouth was at least enjoyable. This time I fancied a battered sausage and chips – wow, the posh life! But I couldn't believe the transformation. Barmouth was heaving, the car parks full, people in the pleasure park screaming... I hated it. I paid £2 to park again, and the queue for the chippy was horrendous, so feeling quite pissed off I bought a hot sausage roll. I drove back to Bala and picked up a takeaway Chinese box for one in the Co-op. Much like Scotland, it's always a Co-op in Wales. But I did get a nice pint of cider in the high street pub before returning to my chalet. After seeing the crowds on Saturday, I decided to stay local on Sunday. It was my last full day before heading home. Breakfast was cereal and Marmite on toast again, and the weather had still not produced the promised sunshine. I decided to drive a circuit of the lake and have a walk. I chose to go around anticlockwise, and found a free parking area that looked to be a twenty minute walk to a café. I walked there along a good pathway, taking in the waterside views and intent on a hot chocolate. But again the queue was huge, so turning tail I headed for Evie. I was becoming quite despondent.

On the quiet southern side of Lake Bala, the road quickly turned into a single track. I was disappointed that the waters could barely be seen from the road; glimpses of the little lakeside railway track could be seen, but I never did catch sight of the actual train, or even any of the stations! Rounding the end of the lake, I saw no point in just driving around aimlessly, so I headed for the Co-op. I had a nice steak in mind for dinner, perhaps with oven chips and salad. There was even a handy pub next-door to the shop; I had a pint of lager for a change. It was Sunday lunchtime, peak time, yet there was just one other customer... it's so sad to see the decline in high streets. I returned to my chalet to read the

Sunday Express with a glass of wine. This would be my last afternoon in Wales; to be honest, I'd be glad to get home. I had yet again hardly spoken to a soul on this trip... I was grateful to have met the pot bellied pig! As for my hosts, not a peep.

Typically, the day of my departure was the best yet, weather-wise. My destination was an inn in a small village near Bourton-on-the-Water, in the Cotswolds. The plan was to get to the inn for lunch, check in, and then visit the quaint little motor museum in Bourton. The first hour driving through mid-Wales, high up in the hills, was spectacular. In the rearview mirror I could see mist hovering in a valley, a perfect photo opportunity. When I pulled over, there was even a sheep grazing by the side of the road. Back in England, the traffic increased, and around Birmingham it became a bloody nightmare. I got to the inn around 1.15pm, looking forward to a pub lunch and a lovely evening meal to round off the trip. But a sign in the pub entrance proclaimed the opening hours, and noted that the bar and restaurant did not open on Sunday evenings, or all day on Monday! I was furious. How could they take the room money in advance and not tell customers this? Their phone number just went to messages, so I left one, got back in Evie, and headed home. I did speak to them the following day, when they refused a refund. Suffice to say, they got a glowing review on Booking.com and Google. Why, oh why, does nothing I try to do ever go to plan?

WOBBLE 6

So now to catch up on recent events, darling. This script could never just be about the travels. I hope that by including my grief journey, it may be a help to others. It's a subject that few talk about, or are prepared for until it suddenly strikes – when you're at your lowest, and are totally unprepared for the hammer blow. I've mentioned this before, but as time goes on, the night time demons have you questioning... Did I do all I could? Did we talk enough? Was I patient enough? And of course there are no answers. It's a living hell. I know you told me to 'have a life'... Ha! There is none without you, Bongle.

Now, a teleconference took place in mid October about the negligence case; still it grinds on. Marianne, our solicitor, a barrister named Jamie, and two medical experts, one a professor, were in attendance. It was scheduled to take two hours. It was my intention to be a bit bolshy, and just say, "Can we just get bloody on with settling this?" Luckily, I took the time to Google the participants... Wow, the barrister had been a negligence specialist since 1999 and the medical men were real experts in Oncology and respiratory cancer.

I was surprised. I learned a lot in those two hours. I didn't like hearing all the terrible medical history again, but the barrister was on the ball, slashing the solicitors' estimate for the claim by around 40%. Now, with a realistic figure to aim for, it just might be over by Christmas. I do hope so, I can't endure this much longer. The sad/funny thing is that by the time it's all over and fees paid, there will not be much more in the coffers than there was to start with! My reckless spending on the promise of the golden compensation carrot has nearly depleted our savings. I know, I'm stupid, but it's just a case of getting through one day to the next. There is no answer for a contented life, my angel.

Last weekend that horrific date, 28th October, rolled around again. Two long bloody years, my dearest, where the hell has it gone? The weather was atrocious, heavy rain and gales. Bruce came over, bless him, and we had fish and chips down at the Beach Bar. It was bonfire night in Littlehampton, with a funfair on the prom, and main car parks all closed. I'd wanted to visit your bench with Bruce. After lunch it was obvious that the evening's events had been cancelled, with the funfair packing up and the no parking signs coming down, so I drove to the car park nearest to your bench and asked the yellow-jacketed attendant if we could park for ten minutes to visit it. The car park was empty, but that jobsworth arsehole still said no!

Gail and Graham invited me in for a wine in the afternoon. I left my watch indoors, so 4.28pm passed without me noticing and reliving that horrible moment of your passing... although I've relived it many nights since. On Sunday I met my sister Kathy for breakfast at the café in the park opposite

Worthing hospital. Not ideal; there are too many memories there, and my mum's wake. They made everyone sit in the gazebo, decorated for Halloween. It was blowing a gale and freezing cold, but the poached eggs were nice. On the Monday, your dear old friend Judy came over, so I took her to see the bench. She was amazed at how lovely our seafront was, even in its stone-strewn post-storm state. She loved the bench. I'd hoped for coffee in the Beach Bar, but it was packed; a bloody inset day. Damn teachers just had a week off for half term. But I did get a seat in the early afternoon, and here I am, bringing everything up to date. I think it will be a long winter my darling. My next trip, a Mediterranean cruise in December, will probably see this book finished. I do hope it makes it into hardcopy, or an eBook... we shall see. I love you, Lin. I miss you.

On Saturday, 4th November, I met up with your family for lunch. Sara, Terry, Ian and Pat, at the Red Lion in Ashington. We had the round table for six in the bay window. We'd sat there before; I had your empty chair next to me, but nobody picked up on it. Two of your favourites were on the menu; sea bass or seafood pasta. I had a chicken burger, not really fancying anything more dramatic. Service was very slow due to a large birthday party group. The conversation was all about their families, their trips past and future, and their plans for Christmas. After two hours, my chest pains and aching neck were causing me discomfort. It seems I have 'severe degeneration' of my neck vertebrae, the cause of my lolling head. Investigations continue. Anyhow, while the others were waiting for their desserts (I didn't order one), Sara said that I looked to be in pain, and should leave if I was uncomfortable. I was happy to escape. I'm afraid they cannot possibly understand how I feel, although I hope they never find themselves in my situation.

I don't want to put a hex on things, but it does look as though your negligence case could be in the final stages. I really do hope so. But it's strange; while I will be relieved, part of me feels it will be another chapter that we endured together, that will be over. Weird.

I've been doing things around the house to pass the time. I fitted a new ceramic kitchen sink, as those awful window fitters knelt on the steel one and stopped it draining. Speaking of the new windows, the right hand one in the bedroom is a pig to open, and during the recent storms a puddle appeared on the windowsill from the damned trickle vents. I am loath to have those Muppets back in the house again though, so I'll sit on it for now.

I have just seen a paramedic nurse at the doctor's, about all my chest and upper body pains. I have an ECG booked on Friday, and a follow up appointment in a couple of weeks.

I'm looking to do a bit of updating in our home; I need a new bed and mattress, but can't decide on the size. Double or single? Probably a small double would be the most practical; the king size is way too big just for me, and is so heavy. The mattress is also coming to the end of the road. The same is true for our reclining chairs in the lounge. I've rotated them, but the cushions aren't like they were. I'll clean them and put them to the sides in the lounge, then get a leather recliner from Careco. They do one rated for twenty-eight stone, god forbid! I've put up a new light in the bedroom. The single candle bulb in the ceiling fan was driving me mad, and the fan is rarely used. I've had thoughts about replacing the kitchen when the money comes through, but then I think, why? It all works, and nobody sees it, so why worry? If any appliances pack up, I'll just replace them. I will get a microwave though, that is looking a bit faded... but then, so am I!

St Barnabus was good today. It was more talk than art, but that's what we all find so good. Only people in our position can understand some of the topics we cover, and it really is therapeutic.

Back to the court case. It looks like we're going to accept £250k; nowhere near the £400k+ first bandied about, but it will put about £160k into our bank, after costs. Enough to provide some security, but not exactly life-changing with today's raging inflation. I can't see me jetting off across the world, unless I lost a shed load of weight, but there is another Arctic cruise in March. It's on Aurora, just like we did in 2020... but would it be too painful? God knows. Otherwise, I'll just top up my premium bonds to the max, and put the maximum allowed into an ISA. Those will be my fall-back reserves, but I really don't want to squander money like I have these last two years.

I do quite fancy a European road trip to all our favourite places; Chiemsee, Salzburg, and of course Spain. Am I up to it? Will I just want to run home? Who knows, because I certainly don't! One step at a time... Focus on the cruise in December. Hopefully it will give me some time to think, with the case over, and to read this and begin to edit it!

I'm increasingly concerned about my chest pains. If my neck vertebrae are deteriorating I could be in real trouble – paralysed even. But just wearing a neck brace could mean the end of driving! Bloody hell. I tried to arrange another appointment with Mr Wolf, the specialist physio at Southlands hospital. It was a nightmare! First I had to ring Worthing hospital, who transferred me to Southlands after twenty minutes. I was told I was

28th in line... So I hung up and sent an email. It's broken Britain at its best! I don't see my GP till the end of November. I say *my* GP, but I've never met him. Should I re-join the gym, to strengthen my upper body and neck muscles, or would that be doing more harm than good? I know that losing a lot of weight would make a huge difference, but that *is* hard. As I get older it does not seem to shift. Even stopping drinking didn't have the usual rapid effect.

I got a cancellation appointment with Mr Wolf. He was impressed with my exercises and said to keep it up. He gave me a direct line number, should my neck get worse. The doctor just upped my blood pressure tablets though...

I've bought three sets of lovely Christmas cards from St Barnabus. I try to support them where possible, as they were so good to you, darling. I got twenty-four 2nd class stamps today; £18, blimey! I hate Christmas now. Last week I gave Paul next-door all our DVDs, and even the player. I can't bring myself to watch our favourite films any more, let alone our Christmas rituals; The Grinch, Miracle on 34th Street, all the various Scrooges... No more, it's too hard. Of course all the decorations are gone, the special ones given to your sister, like your mum's musical Santa. Bruce is doing a family lunch on Christmas Eve, and the neighbours and I have booked a lunch out on Boxing day. That will be quite enough for me. In January I've been toying with the idea of going to Warners on the Isle of Wight. Remember, you sat for hours on their lawn, enthralled by the 'Round the Island' yacht race. We enjoyed our visit, but decided we were ten years too young! Now, old fogey that I am, it would be a good option for a change from Hayling Island. Well, assuming I'm in any fit state to go. I know I want to join you, Bongle, but before that moment, I can't be an invalid. I know that I'm my own worst enemy. I need your guiding hand and voice of reason, as I have always done, my dear. I really dread this winter, and how I might let it diminish me even further. If I can pull myself up a bit, maybe I should have a month in Spain? Pie in the sky, baby. I often had grand ideas – some we actually carried out – but without you, it's a very different prospect.

Today I read that most of Europe has reinstated border guards, due to immigration problems and terrorism. It doesn't really inspire a Grand Tour driving trip! The world is falling apart. I really think that the end of life as we know it is nearly upon us. But it's sparked an idea of how I can carry on writing; sort of, 'Two Clots Ride Again', a book on all our forays down through France to Iberia. First in Pooh the camper in 1994, then in Charlie, our Golf Gti in 1998, and finally in Pooh 2 in 2000, after that damned Hastings nightmare. Plenty of scope there, darling for a lengthy script. It certainly fits the 'Two Clots' billing! Although your astounding memory will be very sadly missed, my dearest Mrs Elephant Head! A trawl through the photo files might help, and there is always 'artistic license'! That cheers me up; something else to do, to pass the long winter. But now, as I'm editing this script, I realise I have pretty much covered those topics... Think again, Coppard!

I had a lovely long chat with Helen O today. She's going to Australia for three months before Christmas to see her daughter, Jeri. She wanted my advice on cruising, as she's booked a two-week cruise around New Zealand while she's out there. She's on the Holland America line. You always wanted to go on the Alaska one from Vancouver... Dammit, we should have done it, and the Rockies rail trip, but we thought we had years. At first it appeared to be really good value; Helen booked a sea view cabin, but is going to upgrade to a veranda, or balcony as we know it. The daily tip of 16 US dollars and the 18% service charge on everything soon boosts the cost though, and it doesn't even look as though there's tea and coffee in the cabin. I think she appreciated all the tips I gave her. I'll probably go to the Suffolk Warners in the spring, and take her for lunch to hear all about it.

The Robin Williams film 'Mrs Doubtfire' has now been made into a stage show, which prompted me to pen another of our adventures... I'm sure you know where I'm going with this, my darling Bongle! It can only be France. We were living in our lovely bungalow in Lancing, and we'd just got a new-to-us car. A silver Nissan Primera Gt, advertised as 'the drivers car,' and it sure was. Half-leather interior, and fast but economical, it was indeed a joy to drive, promoted by the timeless classic 'Silver Machine'. Of course, we named him 'Hawkwind'!

FRANCE IN HAWKIE

A suitable adventure was needed to enjoy Hawkies' driving experience. Northern France would fit the bill; we found an idyllic setting in southern Normandy, a barn conversion in the grounds of the owners' house. Thierry's Barn had a lounge with an open-plan kitchen, comfy leather sofa, and a log burner – perfect for the autumn evenings. Upstairs was a spacious bedroom and bathroom, all low beams and dormer windows with the bed all soft and cosy. We would start the trip with a few days pottering along the coast near our ferry port of Le Havre. Entreat, Fecamp and of course Honfleur would be our overnight stops. We needed to get our ration of Moules et Frites, before moving south for our week in the barn. Portsmouth to Le Havre was only about six hours, so by late afternoon we'd found a room in Entretat. With Hawkie safely parked up, we set off to explore. The town is famous for its eroded chalk cliff to the east, that looks like an elephant dipping it's trunk for a drink. We made it far enough up the cliff path to see the view, before retreating to find a coffee. We found a cosy restaurant for our evening feast of moules, frites, and wonderful crusty baguette to mop up the white wine sauce. We would never tire of this tasty treat.

The next morning we left the hotel, bought croissants and *pain au chocolat*, and in a layby overlooking the cliffs we savoured our crummy (literally!) breakfast. Probably not the best things to eat in a car... A short drive to Fécamp would give us time to visit the *Palais Benedictine,* a museum and home to the aromatic herbal liqueur. It was a most interesting place to wander around; an ancient building with ornate stonework, huge portraits and paintings hanging in the great halls, and giant copper distilling kettles. But the overriding memory for both of us was the aroma from the great mesh storage bins of dried herbs. The recipe of the Benedictine liqueur is still a closely guarded secret. We enjoyed a little tasting session, but we didn't like it enough to buy a whole bottle. Down by the harbour, we had a crêpe from a stall by the sea wall. I told you how, back in the 1970s, there used to be a fast hydrofoil from the then-new Brighton Marina to Fécamp. I used it for a rather disastrous 48-hour trip to Paris – but enough said about that. Good memories only, please! Our hotel was La Frigate, one of my favourites; hopefully room 2, overlooking the quayside. We checked in and settled down for a beer or two. The evening found us wandering the backstreets, where we stumbled upon a super little place and enjoyed the local delicacy called Marmite. We loved it; a rich stew of different types of fish and shellfish in a herby, creamy, white wine sauce, surrounding a tower of rice in the centre of the plate. Coffee and brandy completed this memorable meal. Darling, we were loving this little adventure of ours, and all the more because it was impromptu, with no hotels booked – all in the lap of the gods. We visited Honfleur next, before moving south; this involved driving over the magnificent Pont du Normandy, a stunning piece of engineering spanning the mighty river Seine. It begs the question, if the French can do this, why can't we Brits build a bridge to the Isle of Wight?

We loved Honfleur didn't we, dearest? Staying in hotels or camping on that little site on the riverbank, a stone's throw from town… You know what's coming now, Lin, don't you? I think it must have been in Benny the Bus, around 1998, on our way back from Saumur on the Loire. It was such a shame we sold Benny when we moved to that awful pub in Hastings; remember, we had a little ditty we used to sing as we rolled along? 'Benny the bus, bus is gonna take us, us, over the sea and far away, hahey!' We should have driven him to Italy and forgotten Hastings. But that little campsite, close to lighthouse on the river estuary, was really sweet. Our neighbours, an elderly couple, had an old British Leyland car; a Maestro, I think, and a tiny, ancient-looking caravan. To be honest, the car couldn't have towed anything larger. But they were happy, bless them. They told us they'd been all over Europe with this rig, over the years. As we were looking for a restaurant for the evening, we said hello to them by the inner harbour. He regaled us with another tale of their adventures, pausing many times to say, "Didn't we, Jean?" Thus, we never did know his name – just poor, patient Jean! They were eating homemade sandwiches. We asked them if they'd tried the fantastic local seafood, and he replied, "No, we never eat out, we don't want dysentery now, do we Jean?" We suspected their caravan was full of Heinz baked beans and Fray Bentos corned beef tinned pies! But they were happy – a lesson there, perhaps.

This time, with me having a proper job at last, alongside you at EDF energy, we could afford a nice hotel near the inner harbour. After checking in, we went for an explore and stumbled upon a quirky little museum, the birthplace of Erik

Satie, a famous eccentric French composer. After an enjoyable hour, we found a nice harbour-side table for a beer or two, putting our black hats on and watching the world go by. The evening, as expected was taken up with two portions of Moules a la Normandy with frites and crusty bread. This variation featured crispy lardons and Normandy cider in the sauce. A bottle of cider with the moules was followed by a crisp white wine to linger over with desserts and coffee. Superb!

The next morning, we had a pleasant drive through the Normandy countryside to our gîte. It was surprising how many villages we passed through that had cheeses named after them! We sampled a fair few, too. The gîte was quite rural, with just a village shop and bar a couple of miles away. Thierry greeted us at the gate, with a large hound barking in the background. He showed us around the beautiful property. It was cosy, with a log burner and one free basket of logs – after that, we'd have to get more in the village. Upstairs, the beamed loft was quite wonderful, with dormer windows giving us a view of the night sky from the bed. We'd stocked up at a supermarket on the way in, so were quite set up for a couple of days. We unloaded, I lit the fire, and we sat watching the crackling flames, very contented indeed. There was no internet and only French TV, so we read a lot, which was fine as we'd be out exploring during the day. It seemed like every little town had a châteaux in varying stages of renovation, from crumbling to pristine, many of which were open to the public. We visited one that was under restoration – Château de Beaumesnil, I think it was. That was very interesting, as we were allowed to wander at will. The kitchens are always of great interest, with their blackened hearths and gleaming copper pans. The extensive gardens were in the process of being landscaped; it would be very grand indeed when completed. Our little village bar had a veranda looking over the village, and we tried several types of beer there. The dark *Leffe* was our favourite. If peckish, we had a croque monsieur – a posh name for a cheese and ham toastie! If Thierry was away from home, the damn dog would bark like crazy every time we tried to explore the grounds. Even bribes of ham wouldn't persuade him that we were allowed to be there. Oh well, c'est la vie! One wet afternoon we were housebound, so we delved into the box of DVDs in the lounge. By the roaring fire, with a bottle of wine, we settled down to watch Robin Williams as Mrs Doubtfire – in French! An experience we never forgot, my dearest Linda. We enjoyed a very relaxing week. The country lanes were a joy in Hawkie, our silver machine. The time came to head back to the ferry port – of course, we would factor in time to stock up on wines and cheeses before boarding. Sod's Law being what it is, on the return journey the car starting making an awful screeching, grinding noise. We crawled to a parking area in the next small village. I was going to take the front wheel off the near side, where the noise seemed to be, to investigate... Although how we were going to get a wheel bearing replaced in rural France on a Saturday, I dread to think. Jacking Hawkie up, I grabbed the top and bottom of the tyre to feel the play in the hub bearing. Nothing. So I took the wheel off and examined the brake disc and pads. Turning the hub in the normal, onward direction, a grinding could be heard. Backing it off the other way produced a scrape, and then silence... except for a small piece of gravel dropping from the disc shield! Argh! How bloody annoying. We must have picked it up when we drove on a recently re-surfaced section of road. If I'd just reversed a few yards, the chip would have popped out. Just to round things off, we ran out of time for shopping. My dear, you never said a word. As always, you were so patient with your stupid husband.

CHRISTMAS LOOMING

It's Saturday, 2nd December. My dear, this morning I sat and wrote thirty-odd Christmas cards. That was normally your job; it felt weird doing it. I did wonder if I would send any, but as they're from St Barnabus, I did, as a thank-you and an act of support for them. I'll post/deliver them next Friday, before I go on the next and maybe last cruise. Two years on and I still attend the St Barnabus bereavement art group every fortnight. It's a comfort, strangely. So, I'll be heading for Southampton next week. I think it will be a nice escape, and there's a chance that the damned negligence case could be over by the time I get back. No breath holding on that one, though!

I think this book is just about finished, so I will use the time to review and edit. If I decide that it *is* finished, I want to pay Tony to help make up the covers and get it out on Amazon. I read a couple of pieces out to Gail and Graham, our lovely neighbours, during the week. Damn, Graham had a tear in his eye! They loved it, and enjoyed the writing style. Time will tell, my darling... God I miss you.

I'm sitting with the group in the art room at St Barnabus. I'd intended to start reading and editing, but with everyone chatting it's not really the right place. I'll just have a little wobble on here, and see how it goes. Yesterday the weather was so horrible that I didn't even take the rubbish downstairs. Luckily, a new 1000 piece jigsaw kept me occupied, but it was a long day. The scales revealed that I am not loosing weight. I really have got to get my act together, I'm running out of clothes that fit to take on holiday. I must try to be good on this trip, to skip the cooked breakfast and walk twice round the prom deck every day. I expect I will only use the buffet again. The thought of sitting with a table of seven strangers fills me with horror! You know I always was an antisocial git. Your company was always enough for me… Perhaps that's why I'm finding it so hard to cope? I do hope there are some interesting guest speakers on this trip. Those mid-morning lectures are one of my highlights. I hope I can stay up to see some shows this time, instead of retreating to my cabin to watch Netflix. It will be interesting to see what comes to fruition in the next chapter…

I've been trying to decide what to do about trips in 2024. If the case is not over by then, it won't be a lot. Like my weight, my spending these last two years has been truly wasteful. You'd be so angry, but all I can say is that it's got me through. But it's not sustainable. Perhaps it would do me good just to live on the pensions? I'd still be luckier than most. Speaking to our wonderful neighbour, Patricia, I know I'm not alone in fearing for the future, particularly if my health deteriorates. I'm my own worst enemy, but willpower never was my strong point. You were my rock, and the thought of losing you kept me on the straight and narrow. I've done a lot of soul searching lately, and I have doubts that I'm the nice person I thought I was. Always the questions: was I selfish? Did we talk enough? Was I patient enough? Crazy thoughts, like did you really find your chair more comfortable, or were you just trying to let me get some sleep? I know some readers (if there are any?) may find these thoughts alarming, especially if they're expecting a romantic travel journal. But it's important to log the grief journey, as it's such a taboo subject normally. If only we could talk for a while, I think you would be kind and reassure me that I did all I could. Questions, always the questions, but never answers... And of course, something like this can only be discussed with a true soulmate. And that was you, my dearest Lin.

Now, assuming my funds are replenished – which will also mean that I can dispose of your distressing medical documents and the hundreds of emails – I'll be able to plan some escapes... but not so many cruises. There's only one cruise I've thought about, on Aurora in March. Up to the Artic again, like we did on our last wonderful cruise; happy thoughts, those, and they keep me going. But as usual, a balcony cabin for one is silly money, so it needs some careful thought. Even if the negligence case comes through, it's only half the amount they first intimated. I can't rock the boat, but it does make me mad that huge fees were paid to money men to come up with a figure to aim for, and then the barrister slashes it in half to be realistic – ironically, both their fees are coming out of any settlement! There is so much wrong about these cases. Time, and escalating lawyers' fees for a start, not to mention drawing out the grief and preventing closure on the medical nightmare. Questions really should be raised in parliament.

Ah! It's over! Marianne followed my instructions and sent off the indemnity form. Not complying would have meant going to court. I could see no reason not to sign it and finish the process. She phoned on Friday to say that it could take a month for the funds to come through, but it hasn't really sunk in. I hope I can enjoy the cruise tomorrow, and relax a bit... And even try to plan a life...?

DECEMBER, ON ARCADIA

Boarding at 3pm was a breeze. I even got away with not taking my belt off! It's a real pain to put back on with this hernia. I normally put my belt in with the trousers off, but you can't really do that in the customs hall! I'm in cabin A122, aft, just below the pool bar and buffet. I was pleased to see that Juan Juan is still my steward. I slipped him a tenner to ensure he does my room when I go to breakfast. There's two sea days before Lisbon; it's very rough, storm force ten with six-metre swells in the bay of Biscay, so a tad bumpy. I will do my usual routine of bingo, lectures and some writing. I've got the editing to get to grips with, too. Oh Lin, how I wish you were here with me! Everyone thinks I'm so lucky to keep going away, but they really don't have a clue. It's very hot on the ship. With all the outside doors battened down it's like a ruddy sauna. You know what a grumpy git I am if I'm too hot… and most other times as well, to be honest!

I went to the Crow's Nest bar last night, as my lovely east bar didn't open, despite the Horizon fact sheet saying otherwise. I tried their stock Marlborough wine, 'Wakacrappa' or something like that, to see if it was any better this time. It was not. Stanley the barman (if you believe that's his real name! Why do they make them do this?) said that this prestige bar did have another Marlborough, Villa Maria Sea Breeze special reserve. I said I'd try a small one… for £11.80p! It was nice, though. I had a voucher for a free 'Champagne'; Stanley suggested I put it in the Wakacrappa, as it might make it drinkable. I sipped it, and it was better than expected on its own… so I mixed them together. Now I just had a bigger rubbish drink! Thinking the stainless steel sink in front of me was for washing up, I poured the drink down it, to Stanley's dismay! It contained all the cordial bottles with their pourers fitted… Boy, did I feel an idiot! Stop laughing, Linda! Stanley washed them down with a couple of glasses of water… D'oh! He asked if I wanted another Sea Breeze, and I thought I should… so he poured a large one. £18.40, ouch!

Day three at sea found us still battened down for bad weather. Inside it was hot and stifling… Coppard, do not book any more cruises! It's Lisbon in the morning, so at least I'll be able to walk outside. I've already written about our adventures there, so I doubt there'll be anything new to add. Time to start editing! I've just realised that this cruise is a carbon copy of the one on Ventura, just after your wonderful service – even the same bad weather! It seems like I'm stuck in a never-ending time loop. I've got to break out soon, or perish.

Lisbon is warm and dry, but grey. I can't go ashore, I'd be blubbing my way around all the places we used to stroll hand-in-hand to. I couldn't bear it. I got on board with a casino voucher for £150. It's day four now and I haven't used any of my own money, and have enough chips for two or three more visits. Usually I'm the only one, which shows how antisocial gambling is becoming. That's probably for the best.

Now we're approaching the straights of Gibraltar. Hopefully it'll be sunny once we're in, but it's still grey for now. I washed some clothes out in the cabin yesterday, but will they dry? No. I need a sunny balcony, but I face north on this leg. I'll have sun on the way home, I hope. The daily lectures, normally my favourite activity on board, are all about music, which isn't for me, or obscure battles, full of dates and names, and not really suited to a holiday cruise! Perhaps I should offer to read this to the audience, instead! It's Cartagena tomorrow, and hopefully a stroll ashore. My dear, in truth, I can't wait to get home. What was that sticker we had on the back of our motorhome? 'Adventure before Dementia!' Maybe I need a road trip adventure?

There's been another casualty; two went off in ambulances in Lisbon yesterday, and now, just past Gibraltar, a lady is being helicoptered off. Being on the top deck near the rear pool, we've all been booted out of our cabins! So no shower, and no changing for black tie night. The buffet is closed... it's going to be a long night. Sympathy? No, she arrived late into the darkened theatre, and fell down the stairs. She should have just sat in the disabled seats in the entrance! I found a nice, quiet table to do some editing, and suddenly a family group took all the other chairs and reading became impossible. Now I'm at a desk in the library... at least it's quiet!

Our Cartagena visit was cancelled due to strong winds. Hmm, the forecast only says 16mph. Cost cutting, more likely, so it's two days in Malaga instead. There's a diving team here, cleaning the ship's hull for two days. Cynic that I am, I can't help wondering if Cartagena was ever on the cards. We're in the cruise berths, a fair walk from town, so it will be two long days aboard. I've started going to the gym though, slowly building up the time each day. At least the editing is coming along nicely.

It's the second day now, and I'm sitting by the inside pool, with the sliding roof open at last. There's a little craft group based in the old redundant photo department on deck 2. Today they're using glass pens to do an undersea mural on one of the outside windows around the pool. You would have loved to join in, darling.

Today should have been Gibraltar, but we pushed on to Cadiz. Supposedly it's too windy in Gibraltar... Hmm. That same diving company is here; I suspect they can't work in Gibraltar, and it would have been Sunday when we reached Cadiz... I suspect the captain is telling porkies. We loved Cadiz, but I won't go over that again. There's a chill wind, but it's sunny. I went to the gym again, then sat in the sun for twenty minutes. That's enough for me! I did go for a little walk – saw the sea (ha ha!), some orange trees in a park, and a couple of monuments... but not one open bar or shop. So much for that!

On Sunday, we retraced our course to Gibraltar. I bet the passengers are pissed off, for as we found out, the shops are closed! All we got was a breakfast and a pub lunch. I didn't venture out; it's cold, grey and windy, so much for winter sun! I'll be glad to get home. I played roulette, but I'm getting bored with it. If I cash in my £175 and call it a day, I'll be in profit. It's a sea day tomorrow, so there's a bit more going on, then Vigo – but I won't hold my breath for that, as the visits have so often been cancelled. Another sea day after that, then home!

It's Monday now, and we're at sea. There's two lectures today; the morning one was all about the music and musicians of The Muppets! Wonderful, it actually made me chuckle. You loved it when I laughed, darling. The second, much darker lecture, concerned the speaker's time in the Falklands War.

In the entrance to the main dining room, there's a table of cakes. The chefs have all been competing to make the best Christmas cake, and there's some talented people amongst them; they looked amazing. Twice I tried to play roulette, but there wasn't enough staff to open it as well as the Blackjack table, so I did cash in the chips. If I keep my resolve, I'll have made a profit for a change!

It's Vigo, in northern Spain today. This is our last stop. It's cold, but brighter, and six degrees – cooler than home. I went ashore, briefly. There's a commercial centre, but no supermarket. Damn, I wanted some deodorant! Mine used to last two weeks, but I bet they've cut the contents, just like everything else. I did get a bottle of Brandy in the port shop. Getting back on board, they were confiscating bottles to be given back later! I said, "So we have to go to the shop tonight at 6pm to collect our purchases for packing? What's the point of you taking them for six hours?" And I walked off. I am coming to hate P&O and their jobsworth rules. I had an email from Marianne today; the funds should be in my bank by Friday. Not life-changing, but a comfort blanket. Compensation they call it? As bloody if!

I'm home. It's Thursday, and this book is just about wrapped up now. I hope it will see the light of day at some stage. I fear I'll be a bit lost without my writing. I must think up another angle on our lives, darling, to keep our memories alive. I love you with all my heart. And more than anything, I miss you.

The End

Author's Note

Thank-you so much for downloading and reading my book. I sincerely hope you enjoyed it! If you did, I would really appreciate a review on Amazon - that helps to spread the word, so that others might find and enjoy it.

This book would not have been finished without many hours of help and advice from my friend and mentor, Tony James Slater, whose literary works I have enjoyed for years. Thank-you for making *Two Equals One* a reality.

My journey through grief is a long and ongoing process. If you are in the same boat, dear reader, then my heart goes out to you. Please know that you are not alone, and feel free to get in touch.

You can reach me at: twoclots@gmail.com

Best wishes,

Steve Coppard